NO MORE
FRIENDLY
FIRE

Ending the gender war in the Church

HELEN & TIM ROBERTS

RIVER
PUBLISHING

River Publishing & Media Ltd
info@river-publishing.co.uk

ISBN 978-1-908393-78-4
Cover design by www.spiffingcovers.com

CONTENTS

What Others Are Saying About This Book

What a refreshingly honest and practical read *No More Friendly Fire* is. In the introduction Tim and Helen make the statement that this book is "not about marriage, but about partnership". They have co-led Wellspring Church in Watford for over 19 years and write from this rich experience. They tackle theology and go beyond it. They are honest about their challenges and share their dream for a better future – women and men working as equals, in partnership serving God's purposes. A must read!

Billy Kennedy, Senior Leader, New Community Church (Southampton), Leader, Pioneer Churches (UK), President, Churches Together in England

Our neighbourhoods, cities and nations will only be transformed into all that God wants them to become when we truly embrace difference and diversity. I wholeheartedly recommend Tim and Helen's book.

Matt Bird, Founder of Cinnamon Network International

Helen and Tim have emphasised the beauty of good partnership in Christ between women and men, whether married, colleagues or partners in the Gospel. They also help us to understand some of the tensions which can arise when the gender issues of the world we live in corrode the relationships God intends for us in Christ. It is particularly moving when the authors speak of their personal journeys and their need to face issues, and struggle at times to get to that place where God desires us to be. A new perspective on an ancient theme of God – women and men.

Dianne Tidball, President of The Baptist Union of Great Britain

Once you know the Father's heart for all his children, male and female alike, then you will know why it is so important for them to partner together to extend the Kingdom of God on this earth. Tim and Helen's very readable book is insightful, powerful and includes the testimony of their personal faith journey. I highly recommend it.

Ron Corzine, Founder of Christian Fellowship International (USA)

Tim and Helen Roberts don't just talk about men and women in leadership, they live it. They are a great example of a husband and wife dream-team who complement each other brilliantly. This book is honest, challenging and will stretch your thinking – we know that's what it did for us!

Matthew and Becky Murray, Founders and Directors, One By One.

Tim and Helen provide us with a key component in the "gender in ministry" debate – that of the collaboration and partnering of men and women in work/ministry and leadership. In recent years, much has been done to establish women in their equality and God-given roles and destinies. *No More Friendly Fire* seeks to address some of the relational dynamics that follow this transition. Tim and Helen have walked the challenges of this pathway together and model the message of their writing in real life, alongside a healthy marriage and family. Their vulnerability and integrity shine through these pages.

Peter and Mariette Stott

No More Friendly Fire is both carefully and passionately written to show how men and women can lead together. It is both biblical and practical, prophetic and kind. It is also an urgent call to the Church to not just talk about women in leadership, but in a much greater way to model a leadership that is inclusive. This book is not written in an ivory tower. Helen and Tim have modelled this brilliantly for years as they have led

Wellspring Church in Watford. Learn from their struggles and mistakes, honestly shared. Above all, be inspired to dream of what could be. A great book from two great ministers of the Gospel who have learned what it is to be team.

Mike Pilavachi, Co-Founder and Leader, Soul Survivor

Helen and Tim Roberts provide an important roadmap for every Christian and leader who wants to navigate the space between heritage and baggage on one of the vexed issues of our time. The question of gender roles continues to prove hazardous for some sections of the Church. In the space of a generation, attitudes have shifted significantly in the wider culture. Yet some Christians struggle to marry the changes they see with the biblical record, sometimes with just cause. Helen and Tim address gender roles forthrightly and intelligently – and without the sensationalism that often goes with this territory. While happy to share lessons learned from their experience as co-leaders of a very exciting church, their central focus is always the biblical record. This book will make you think and it will inspire you to challenge the status quo in line with Bible truth.

Mal Fletcher, Founder and Chairman, 2020Plus think tank, London

This is an essential read and call to action for all leaders. This narrative presents how misinterpretation of the Word of God to accommodate man's ideal of gender and roles can inadvertently cause damage and hurt, which the authors describe as "friendly fire". Inspired by God and presented in a style that is unambiguous, the reader will benefit from Tim and Helen's approach which addresses a potentially contentious subject, and demonstrates how being trapped in tradition can be debilitating for both women and men. Through exposure of the potentially damaging results of inequality and attitudes that exist within the Church, this book provides an opportunity for us to actively respond and utilise our individual, unique, God-given gifts and purpose in the kingdom of God.

You will be enticed not only by a good read, but if you are willing, you will change your perceptions, challenge your traditional thinking, practice and ideals. I therefore encourage prayerful reflection and a willingness to understanding how our roles and gender can impact on all relationships in a positive way.

Dr Angela F Herbert MBE, FSET

Being born a woman will never be seen as a disadvantage when we understand that she not only carries and reflects the image of God, but in the womb of the first woman, she was made to be fruitful, to subdue the earth and rule all creation. Living under the authority of heaven, man and woman were created and called to walk side by side, so that through their partnership they would both complete and complement each other.

This is the passionate message of the book before you, as Tim and Helen not only unpack their personal journey with vulnerability and sensitivity, but engage with the heart of the Scriptures to capture the original intention of the Creator: to release His creation into the fullness of their potential and purpose. The cry of this book is that whatever we have become, in and through Jesus we can return to the Lord's pre-fall dream: that His image, both male and female, would work together as one for His glory.

Dr John Andrews, Author, Leader and Teacher

Helen and Tim Roberts herald a resounding call to end the gender war in the Church by following God's plan for partnership between men and women in sharing his love and truth. Delving into the Bible and their own stories of leadership, they make a winsome case for unity in a combined purpose. Read this book to be bolstered in your faith – and empowered for ministry!

Amy Boucher Pye, Author of *Finding Myself in Britain*

DEDICATION

To Bethany, Hannah and David. May you abound in the freedom Jesus fought for and become all he created you to be.

ACKNOWLEDGEMENTS

To our three amazing kids, thank you for helping us in so many ways to write this book. Dinnertime conversations have challenged us to make sure we practise what we preach and live out what we write.

For all those who read the earliest manuscripts and have not given up on this project, we are thankful – especially John Andrews, Brett Jordan, Robin Sanderson and Rebecca Palmer for reading and re-reading and cheering us on all the way.

Thanks also to Cathy Davenport for your eager eagle-eye and your enthusiasm for what we've written.

To our incredibly faithful church family – all of you in Wellspring Church have in some way helped us become who God is calling us to be. You have helped shape us and this message and we are so thankful. We pray that the church and communities we love will be healthier as a result, now and for future generations.

Finally, massive thanks to Tim Pettingale and the River team for catching the heart behind this years ago and bringing it to a wider audience. God bless you!

Foreword

When we first met at Bible College (yes *London Bridal College* as it was nicknamed back then), we did not instantly fall in love but began a journey of friendship together. We quickly realised that there were significant differences between us, but that at the same time we shared a desire to do all we could for the Kingdom and to both fulfil our potential in Christ, whatever that turned out to be.

Later, as our romance deepened, there was a sense of knowing that God was calling us to "prefer one another" and to love one another more than we loved ourselves. We would sit for hours chatting and praying in the college "quiet room" next to chapel, becoming increasingly aware that our future was about releasing every bit of potential that we possible could – not just in ourselves, but in one another.

The reality is that, as kids come along and the crazy teenage ideals are challenged, you realise that you have to work harder to think of "self" less and to keep choosing to "deny yourself and take up your cross and follow Jesus" (Matthew 16:24).

When one of us is off roaming the country preaching and seeing the Lord move in power, the other will be at home with the dirty laundry, sibling rivalry and meals to cook, and self-pity unconsciously creeps in! However, we do believe that Jesus has called us *both* to give everything that we have to serve Him wherever, whenever and whatever the cost. Sometimes there are more "out there" seasons and sometimes the ministry focus is more at home. Everything we do for God pleases Him and no one role, job, or title is more important to Him – even though the world would tell us otherwise.

In this book, Tim and Helen write in such an insightful way regarding their journey through these challenges and numerous others too. Their heart is totally centred on releasing one another to fulfil their potential but, in the midst of that, they acknowledge and address the real issues between the sexes, from a Church perspective and from the Bible. They speak helpfully from their own experiences of navigating the ministry playing field and how to overcome the attacker, in order to score a Kingdom goal. Their focus is not on self-promotion, but on promoting Jesus and they are committed to doing and being all they can in Him to faithfully work out their call.

The reality is that there are stereotypes in the Church and at times it is difficult for a woman to find a place to grow. As Helen helpfully and vulnerably observes, we have to learn how to walk humbly and yet know when to speak up boldly. The balance in this is something she helps us to find. Tim's words help to open our eyes and ears to a male perspective and to changes we can make to release one another more. We all need people to champion us in the roles we have been given; particularly in leadership.

This book has made us think again as the Roberts' sensitively challenge some of the accepted conflict that has gone on for too long between the sexes in the Church. God made men and women to serve together, grow together and live together. Tim and Helen expose many of the issues, suggest possible new ways forward, and make a significant contribution. It is easy to read, engagingly written and delicately enlightening.

This book is not just for couples. All of us face times and situations in which conflict between the genders limits what the Lord can do in and through us. We need to learn to get along better, to release one another, and to realise that we are all part of one body. Get hold of this book and let the challenge, wisdom and insight it contains empower you to better see the Lord work powerfully across the gender divide.

Gavin and Anne Calver

INTRODUCTION

Taking time to read this book is like hitting the pause button on a powerful war epic. Think of Tolkien's *Lord of the Rings* or the *Narnia* movies inspired by C.S. Lewis. There is chaos, carnage and confusion everywhere on this battlefield and you begin to wonder which side is winning, or indeed who is fighting who, as each blow is shown in slow motion and the violins underscore the tragic, personal loss of life; the loss of hope. Another blow, another body recoiling in pain, crashing to the ground, perhaps never to stand again.

Pause.

Alright, maybe it isn't quite that dramatic with blood and dismemberment, but you get the idea. In recent generations massive strides have been made in Western society towards the emancipation of women, gender equality and the dignifying of all people, regardless of their sex. There is still a long, long way to go, but we thank God for progress and for the authenticity of laws and institutions that have been changed or established to reinforce the equality of men and women.

This book is not about that. This is about the Church we dream of; the one we want to hand on to our grandchildren. It is about your church and ours, and the way men and women are called to live, love, and serve Jesus together. We want to take you on a journey of discovery towards a brighter future in the Church, where gift comes before gender, where women and men are equally valued, listened to, and are as free to develop and use their gifts.

This book is for those who have seen the scars and felt the pain of the battle of the sexes in the body of Christ – where in too many instances men have held on to power, and too often women have been forced to compete for influence and position. This is for you, if you have wondered what kind of Church we are handing over to the next generation. As church leaders since the late 1990s we have walked this journey, had these fights and wrestled with these issues in a context of relative freedom, compared to most. Even within this context, we have faced within ourselves, within our marriage and within our church, a stockpile of incendiary attitudes, mind-sets and theologies that have proved explosive and potentially calamitous.

By God's grace we have navigated the theatre of this war to get to this point. The reason for pausing is to encourage those around us to think again, in light of Scripture, about the role of men and women, and of God's redeeming plan to unite us in authentic partnership. Even after more than twenty years in Christian leadership we still have a hope in our hearts that things can and will be different; that the Western Church can express more fully the kingdom of God on the earth.

We are writing this for you, so you can find clarity and gain wisdom from heaven to walk your own path, avoid hidden mines and, more importantly, consciously avoid damage to fellow soldiers – to comrades in what we are called to: a war against evil.

Men, this book is for you because there is still so much to learn about serving the women in your life, and in the Church, authentically, strongly and confidently; encouraging them to be victorious as we face a common enemy. For far too long we have held on to positions of influence, putting gender before gift and, as a result, have hampered the health and growth of the Church.

Women, this book is also for you. The men you know, who you are called to "fight the good fight" alongside, are not your enemy. The devil of division has caused enough pain for us all; we will do well to focus our fight on him and ask for grace to abound again within the Church. We believe this book will help you to see even more clearly how you are invited by God to play an equal part in restoring his Kingdom rule on the earth. As you fight with the strengths God has given, you can do so while embracing the strengths of the men he has called along with you.

This book is not about *marriage*, it is about *partnership*. We'll be exploring some powerful, history-making and future-shaping partnerships between men and women who were not married, but in their working together God used them to push back the enemy and defeat his evil schemes of division. You will be inspired and encouraged to see that God's agenda, supremely and ultimately worked out on the cross of Christ, was to restore humanity with self-emptying, selfless love. He died to reverse the curse that started the war between Adam and Eve and has affected every generation since. Christ came to dignify human relationships again. To restore them to the point where, with God at the centre of it all, each member's contribution, gifts and qualities are celebrated, regardless of gender.

Our prayer and desire is that we might spare you some of the pain we have experienced and, more importantly, help the Western Church find greater freedom for men and women to fight together, rather than fighting each other. We are calling a ceasefire, blowing a trumpet, to say "enough is enough". Men and women can and should walk, live and serve alongside one another in the Church as we face the tyrant of evil with confidence, together.

Perhaps we'll be stirring up some deep emotions, some real regrets and some strong opinions? We all have tucked away some deeply-held suspicions and fears about how men and women should live, love and serve in the Church. It's time to take an honest look at why we believe what we do, and what beliefs have inspired our often questionable behaviour. We may be afraid to let go of power or position, sharing our influence, platform or authority. Men, women, let's talk about that... We may be more inclined to undermine, subvert and manipulate those in power, or those who have what we want. Jealousy can be so powerful and rebellion can bring ruin. Let's be honest about this and consider new ways of thinking and living, together.

We'll start by surveying the battle scene, taking an honest look at where we've got to, who has been hurt and why. Then we'll look at some inspiring examples of male-female biblical partnerships that shaped our history, before looking at Jesus and how he loved and empowered the women he served alongside. Before we finish we'll consider Paul's remarkable and challenging teaching about gift and gender and we'll discover in it all some new perspectives on this centuries-old conflict.

You may be able to guess who has written each section or chapter, and in some cases it has been necessary to indicate this clearly. That said, what you have here is the result of many years of serving, leading, reading, study and writing together, where our thoughts have (mostly) intertwined. We have thrown our all into compiling and ordering what we have learned so far, to help you explore your own perspectives, ask your own questions and, God-willing, find your own peace in how you relate to those around you. May heaven's unity bring blessing in your world.

Thanks for joining us as we step over the ruin and rubble caused by those who have gone before us. We can face the future with restored dignity and renewed confidence in our victorious Christ, who calls his followers to live in the light of a curse that has been reversed, a battle that has been won, and an eternal kingdom where men and women are on the same side.

As we step out on this journey of thought and exploration,

let's keep a dream alive. Imagine a Church that leads the way in our communities by showing dignity to all, embracing and developing God-given talent and skill, regardless of gender; a Christian community where sexism is an embarrassing thing of the past and our grand-daughters are as likely and free to lead as our grandsons. Regardless of denomination and tradition, imagine what kind of blessing across the body of Christ would be experienced if the war between us as men and women was history. It is God's desire, surely, that we pursue this vision with determination and faith, that our history need not be our future. To this end, and with open hearts, let's press on.

Section 1: Setting the Scene

A friend of ours once pointed out a simple profundity: You can only get to where you want to be from where you are (not where you wish you were). In this section we'll survey the scene of the gender war in the Church and beyond.

As you read this, you might not have experienced yourself the harsh realities we'll describe. It may not be your story. You might not even be aware of how things are for others. Nevertheless, if we are going to reach the destination where men and women are released according to their gifts, we would be wise to acknowledge what has happened on this battle scene hitherto.

CHAPTER 1
MR AND MRS SMITH AND THE FOG OF WAR

The battle of the sexes is raging all over the world, and has been for millennia. Where war sets in, there forms a malaise – a destructive commotion of blood, sweat and wreckage. In this context we can lose our sense of what's right, who is where, where our enemy is. Between men and women this can lead to one-upmanship, further pain, bloodshed and heartache. In fact, longer lasting than any other battle in history is the fight between men and women.

Perhaps this particular struggle has escaped you and yours. Maybe those you love have escaped any damage? If that's the case, wonderful! We still urge you to read on, however, as for many people in the world, notably in the Church, a new vision is needed where men and women fight strongly *alongside* each other against a common enemy.

As we embark on this mission together, you may well get the impression we are writing out of a lot of painful experiences, arguments and tension. That's kind of true. We have worked through a lot, and we have learned so much over the years of living, loving and leading together. The fruit of some of that is ripe and ready, and forms the basis of this book. We have come through a number of battles, but nothing like *Mr and Mrs Smith*.

Inspiration for sermons and books can come from the most unlikely sources, not least from Hollywood. One evening we sat down to watch *Mr & Mrs Smith*, starring Angelina Jolie and Brad Pitt. (Before you rush to see this film, be warned there are significant scenes of domestic violence and this chapter should come with a "spoiler alert". Having established that, read on, brave one…). Brad and Angelina play a couple who are both highly successful assassins, working for two independent, rival companies. They happen to meet mid-mission and form a relationship which results (one thing leading to another, as it does) in them getting married. Quite possibly it is a marriage of convenience as it gives each of them, unbeknown to the other, a legitimate cover for their alternative employment. Of course, looking like they do, along with convenience comes an explosive dose of physical attraction! However, the attraction and convenience are not enough to help them build a deep relationship. Boredom sets in. The cracks in their marriage begin to show. It all takes on a new dimension when each of them receives the same assassination assignment. Not realising the involvement of their spouse, they set about fulfilling their mission. Obviously, their mutual involvement complicates the mission as their companies, realising the status of their relationship, set them an assignment to silence the opposition and assassinate one another! With humorous and tragic consequences their mission is thwarted and the dawn rises on what is actually going on. They realise who their *real* enemy is. They must call an end to friendly fire.

Mr and Mrs Smith are not each other's enemy. But they still have to fight. Together. To turn and face their common enemy. There is a humorous wardrobe-choice in one of the pivotal scenes when the two assassins find themselves sitting with their only remaining friend, both wearing jackets embroiderd with the words "Jesus Rocks". They are discussing whether they want to leave each other and have a chance of staying alive or stay together and take on the real enemy, risking their own deaths. They had come to realise a genuine love for each other and therefore their choice was not simple or straightforward (it rarely is). Recognising their real enemy, they move forward together. In a beautifully Hollywood-choreographed shoot-out, they cover each other's backs and are the only ones who walk out alive, their enemies defeated.

It's hard to miss the spiritual parallels for the sexes in the Church today. The reality dawns that the battle between male and female is very real, deadly at times. Even when no actual blood is being shed, gifts and talents are hitting the deck and being left for dead. The stakes are high. Sadly, it is in our fighting with each other that we are kept busy from fighting our real adversary. There appears to be a price on our heads. Christian men and women are on hell's hit-list and division is their goal. Our enemy wants us to fight each other instead of fighting together. But we do so at our own peril, distracting us and blindsiding us again and again.

There in a nutshell is the premise of this book and we invite you to join us as we share from our own story, and from the stories of men and women in the Bible, to explore what this looks like in our everyday lives, here and now.

Tim writes:

It was my second sabbatical, the first week, and a number of factors compounded to bring Helen and I both to breaking point. We ended up at war with each other, a skirmish that was more intense than ever, a battle thankfully that we both won. We stared into an abyss we had not encountered before. In all our years of serving together, in over 20 years of marriage and 14 years of co-leading our church, I'm not sure we had ever been to the point of wanting to walk away from the whole shebang at the same time. We had ridden the crest of a wave and then the wave crashed onto the beach with pebbles and marine debris flying in every direction!

I'd just been given a civic award by the Mayor of Watford,

our leadership team and church were cheering us on as I took a 3-month break to study, pray, travel and write, and things were looking rosy. So we went into this battlefield with our guard down. We had relatives staying in our house so we were sleeping on the sofa, in the lounge. Joy! Then there was the intensity of "de-pressurising" that comes with the first few days of sabbatical, let alone the transfer of responsibility with Helen taking on all of my ministry burdens as well as her own. We faced a fight we should have seen coming. We laugh now, but we were scowling then. We decided we would independently journal our daily thoughts and emotions, agreeing that we would compare notes to help us adjust and understand each other. A few days went on, pressure mounted, dark thoughts about leaving each other were crossing both our minds and finding their way onto our journal pages.

"Maybe you shouldn't read my journal just now!" Helen said. I was so relieved! In those rare few days I was convinced Helen was against me. What I had written was also unreadable! We were becoming enemies.

I can't honestly recall how things turned, or a specific moment when we recovered our commitment to strengthening our unity. What I do know is at some point we came to realise something profound: *We were on the same side.* The Devil of Division had managed to turn us against each other, and what a dark place that is to visit. Lies fuel vitriol, and even a few days' unforgiveness fuels division. When our guard is down it's so easy to find ourselves fighting the wrong enemy... so help us, God!

Between men and women, even in the Church, lies are like bullets flying past us at an alarming rate and being sent from every direction. What will it mean for us to wake up to the call for equality and unity? Can we wake up to the reality that while we are fighting each other the enemy is winning? It is time to turn and, instead of stabbing one another in the back, face the enemy side-by-side.

Tim's dad and uncle are Vietnam War veterans and experienced some traumatic things as a pilot and soldier in what turned out to be an almost pointless war in South East Asia. The memories and scars of the battlefield remain vivid. So too with other members of our families and indeed our church family who will never forget their first-hand experience of wartime. However, for most of us our knowledge of actual front-line war is shaped by the media, through news, films, articles and books. Few of us will know people who have been into active war zones and even fewer will have personal experience of it. Whilst hundreds of thousands of teenagers spend countless hours on *Call of Duty* or similar games in the comfort of suburban bedrooms, we can all appreciate that real war is so much deeper than our TV screens. Even as we write, the battles continue on Syrian streets in a nation which has a multitude of enemies all claiming supremacy. The situation is so complex that Western powers are confused about who to back, who to fight for and against, and whose cause is the most genuine. War is brutally conflicting.

There are so many aspects of uncertainty in war that a term was coined by a Prussian military analyst Carl Von Clausewitz in the book *On War*, posthumously published in 1873. He used the phrase "the fog of war". Clausewitz said, "War is an area of uncertainty; three quarters of the things on which all action in war is based are lying in a fog of uncertainty to a greater or lesser extent. The first thing needed here is a fine, piercing mind, to feel out the truth with the measure of its judgment."[1]

Knowing the enemy's strengths, capabilities and intentions combined with a soldier, or unit's awareness of their own strengths, capabilities and intentions can nevertheless lead to an escalating ambiguity and misunderstanding about anticipated mission objectives. Confidence and certainty can give way to confusion very quickly in war environments. Holding on to essential truths, fixed navigation points and a clarity about the mission's purpose is essential to avoid defeat.

It is this layer-upon-layer of uncertainty that leads to the so-called "fog of war", where truth and clarity seem camouflaged and undetectable. If you've ever tried to drive a car through intense fog you will know the threatening feeling of uncertainty of where the road is. Neither safety nor perils can be detected.

One of the apparent dangers in a battle scene is when there is a fog of war that envelops the fighters – when there is so much noise, gunfire, movement and activity that no one really knows what is actually going on or who is doing what. It is in this melee that the chance of friendly fire rapidly escalates. This is when it is difficult to recognise whether someone is friend or foe. This is where avoidable fatalities occur.

Injuries and loss are an inevitable risk in any war. However, the death of innocent civilians carries far greater regret than the loss of those engaged in the battle. Furthermore, creating casualties of war from members of an army's own unit, from their own side, is devastating. So too between us, men and women. We can see the wreckage wrought by our in-fighting that has resulted in countless casualties. Unnecessary casualties. In homes, schools, colleges, workplaces and churches today, we have become confused about: Who are we? What is the role of men and women? Is it different or the same? What is equality and does it matter? Is this all men's fault? So many questions. That is why we write: So the fog may clear and from the resulting clarity, we might see in reality a vision of greater freedom and peace for our communities.

So, where are we at in that war today? That's where we will turn to next…

Chapter 2
Women – victims of friendly fire

One influential book we've read in recent years is that written by husband and wife journalistic-team Nicholas D. Kristof and Sheryl Wudunn called *Half the Sky*. The book's title is derived from Chinese proverb saying *women hold up half the sky*. It is a gripping, heart-breaking, essential read. In the words of the authors, their reason for writing was to recruit their audience to "join an incipient movement to emancipate women and fight global poverty by unlocking women's power as economic catalysts. This is the process under way – not a drama of victimisation but of empowerment, the kind that transforms bubbly teenage girls from brothel slaves into successful businesswomen. This is a story of transformation. It is change that is already taking place, and change that can accelerate if you'll just open your heart and join in."[2]

There seems to us to be a significant tension across the globe regarding the gender battle. In the Western world, glass ceilings are said to restrict women from rising as far as men and, furthermore, salaries for similar roles are disproportionately divided. In too many cases women are overlooked for opportunities. Gender gaps exist within the worlds of sports, politics, business, entertainment and many other professions – even in the Church – fuelling the fire of gender disparity. Surveying the global picture of gender inequality, you don't have to look too far to realise that there are way too many occasions when the discrimination becomes lethal. Kristof and Wudunn report that the "global statistics on the abuse of girls are numbing. It appears that more girls have been killed in the last fifty years, precisely because they were girls, than men were killed in all the battles of the twentieth century. More girls are killed in this routine 'genocide' in any one decade than people were slaughtered in all the genocides of the twentieth century. In the nineteenth century, the central moral challenge was slavery ... (they) believe that in this century the paramount moral challenge will be the struggle for gender equality around the world."[3]

With every unfolding tragedy reported by Kristoff and Wudunn, they do not seem to be bringing God into the solution. In fact, God is often shown in a very bad light, or at least his people are. As these stories are told, it is hard to see where hope is coming from. Then this...

"If there is to be a successful movement on behalf of women in poor countries, it will have to bridge the God Gulf. Secular bleeding hearts and religious bleeding hearts will have to forge a common cause. That's what happened two centuries ago in the abolitionist movement, when liberal deists and conservative evangelicals joined forces to overthrow slavery. And it's the only way to muster the political will to get now-invisible women onto the international agenda..."

Kristoff and Wudunn conclude that,

"...it is particularly crucial to *incorporate Pentecostalism* into a movement for women's rights around the globe [we're sitting up now!] because it is gaining ground more quickly than any other faith… (Whilst some) regard the Pentecostal boom with some suspicion (because of false promises for divine favour) without doubt it also has a positive impact on the role of women. Pentecostal churches typically encourage all members of the congregation to speak up and preach during the service. So for the first time, many ordinary women find themselves exercising leadership and declaring their positions on moral and religious matters."[4]

Helen writes:

As one of those "ordinary women" I am part of a Pentecostal movement; one of the largest in the world – Assemblies of God GB. I'm thrilled that these journalists have observed that we teach, practise and advocate (in part) our belief that women can serve in any role and ministry. Churches are led by men, women, or husband-and-wife teams, or larger mixed teams. However, there are still tensions and we have not, in my opinion or experience, gone far enough in recognising the gender inequalities which perpetuate the problem rather than facilitating transformation. A lot of damage has been done and it is time for us to wage peace; to fight this inequality together.

I have observed a wide-ranging avoidance of men mentoring women from both sides of the gender divide. In other words, many men avoid this, as do some women. The motivation is not intentionally harmful, but rather is fuelled by a desire to be wise, cautious and without reproach. However, I would suggest that in the mix of motivation there is also an essence of fear. This means that male leaders only mentor male emerging-leaders, unless the wife of the leader is there for protection; as if this would be a failsafe protection for their apparently fragile purity. This is a safety-measure which intrinsically hampers the development of women leaders. The fear of moral failure can grip people. This is understandable to a point, in light of recent high-profile scandals and exposés of power-games and sexual misdemeanours. I've been around leaders long enough to see the damage on families, churches and networks when a leader falls into a spiral of emotional and sexual unfaithfulness. So, perhaps to avoid this at all costs, a fear of failure can be presented as God-given wisdom to protect against the temptation of adultery. Of course, in pastoral situations wisdom is needed in this area, but I am talking about leadership development. We can become so afraid of doing something wrong we fail to do something right. Men exclusively mentoring each other can perpetuate a jobs-for-the-boys stronghold, limiting women from growing and developing in their gifting, and reducing opportunities to express those gifts from platforms of influence.

A resulting challenge means that women can become embittered, resentful and even rise up with anger in their hearts, trying to take what they perceive should be theirs. Extremes of feminism can be just that – extreme! None of which would be necessary if we were loving one another with a selfless, self-emptying love; a love which prefers others.

There are so many important and timely aspects to this discussion, not least in the area of gender definition and sexuality and the gradual and pervasive move towards the redefinition of marriage by even the most conservative Western governments. In this environment of liberalisation and "progressive" social restructuring, the language of equality has become confused. In some cases our societies are embracing the whole spectrum of diverse sexuality types and identities. An ever-increasing series of categories is discovered as teen culture embraces ambiguity. At the same time we are in an age where too often unity is seen as uniformity. God-given sex differences are being underplayed and we identify a major trend towards undermining any clear distinctions at all. This is an important dialogue, but not the primary focus of what we are writing here.

The focus of this book is not about gender equality alone, nor about women in leadership, but rather the relationship between men and women, and the compelling invitation of the Bible to work in powerful partnership.

The enemy loves seeing the Church turn in on itself. When we are distracted by in-fighting, much like Mr and Mrs Smith in the movie, we don't have time to fight the real enemy. So called *friendly fire* can result in spiritual impotency. Instead of breaking through barriers, it builds new ones. It is time for a trumpet call that ends the battle of the sexes, so that we must turn and face the enemy of division. In modern warfare friendly fire is avoided at all costs as it destroys morale and increases division amongst allies. Between men and women, not least in the Church, we can inadvertently hurt those we are destined to love. It's time to wage peace in the battle between male and female.

In the Western world, in Pentecostalism, we have been given so much. We have undeserved favour and opportunity. We believe now is the time to establish a renewed collaboration between men and women. We can work together in today's world to see wider transformation. Can the working together of male and female display God's glory and purposes more fully to bring an end to gender-inspired atrocities? Are we living in the freedom and completed work of the cross? Or are we, as believers, still living in the implications and consequences of "the curse"[5] when it comes to relationships between men and women?

To be able to use the opportunities available to us in order to end worldwide gender atrocities, to have a voice into our communities, and to have permission to contribute to this significant discussion, we must be sure to not be hypocrites at home. We have to ensure our house is in order and as Christians we have a great responsibility to make sure there is no proverbial log in our own eye.

We are writing to identify the real enemy; raising our voices together with a cry for deeper transformation. The working together of male and female can uniquely display God's glory and purposes. So, let's put an end to the collateral damage in the lives of those around us, and take our lead from the inspiring biblical relationships examined in the chapters to come. As we do this with increased clarity and focus, we can imagine and build a stronger Church, and a wider society that will serve our grandchildren well, providing a context of selfless love and mutual respect, partnership and unified diversity.

Implications and application – some questions

- As you survey the wreckage from your own standpoint, with your own experience of life in the Church, what are the main implications for Christian communities if the gender war is allowed to continue?
- What do you think are the implications for the future of society as a whole?
- As you consider your own personal experiences, how have you personally been complicit in the wrong kind of fighting, or seeing others in the church as your enemy, especially those of the opposite sex?
- How would you suggest influencers and leaders in your part of the Church can respond to this – what should they say or do to arrest the gender war?

A prayer

Loving Father, you know and see all things. Thank you for loving us anyway!

We are all your sons and daughters and we ask you to show us what you see. By your Holy Spirit, reveal to us where humility and grace are needed in greater measure among your people. Reveal to us things that are hidden, even bringing into your light those painful memories and sins we find difficult to talk about or admit. We ask you to refine us like silver, that we will radiate the Father's glory in the name of Jesus.

And, our dear Saviour, thank you for giving your life so we can be part of your eternal family, enjoying the closeness and joy of heaven here on earth, amongst your people – the Church you love so dearly. Your body was broken so we could be made whole, together.

Loving God, teach and lead us for your glory here and now, and forever.

Amen.

SECTION 2: WHAT WENT WRONG?

As we've already established, somewhere along the way we've gone off course from how we imagine things could and should be between men and women in our world. Instead of a garden of dignity we have a battlefield of broken hearts. Surely this is not how we were designed to be by a loving God.

In this section we will go back to the beginning of it all, the Creation story, and see where our journey began to veer away from the divine design.

Chapter 3
In the Beginning: Unity in Diversity

We can't wait to share with you some of our insight from the Bible about how we can fight, together, in our everyday lives. Whether married or single, whatever your age, you are on your way to making some (perhaps) new and (for sure) exciting discoveries about how we can win the gender battle that threatens the peace of our communities.

Starting a movie or a book halfway through is never a great idea. Starting at the beginning is the only way to really understand the author's thread. So let us go back to the very beginning of creation and look again at some of the most well-known stories. We know this will be familiar to many, but stick with us because we think we have something fresh to say.

In Genesis we have both an overview synopsis and a more detailed account of how it all began. God has five phenomenal days as he demonstrates his creative genius, preparing the environment, the landscapes, the sights, sounds and smells of the earth; designing and forming creation from the depths of his imagination and spreading it to the corners of the globe. The Lord's pleasure is apparent as the plethora of divinely-designed beauty unfolds before his eyes as he, the Master Craftsman, produces and positions his multi-dimensional expression of creation. Imagine the colours and the smells of the all that is green, floral and fruitful before you. Imagine the sounds of the plants moving in the wind, the chorus of birds and animals at dawn, the trickling waters making their way from the spring.

Then, on day six, the triune God – Father, Spirit, Son – created both male and female, unlike anything crafted to date, to be a reflection of him. In perfect unity and community, a glorious reflection of the divine. Unblemished. Glorious. Is this reflection like a mirror-effect so that God gazes upon humankind and sees himself? Or is it like a parent who looks at their child and sees aspects of themselves staring right back at them? What a mystery. This the inspiration of countless tomes and the most beautiful psalms and songs of praise. We were created by glory, for glory.

In this mysterious act of creation, humankind was expressed as being both male and female. In other words, the reflection of the Creator was expressed not in a blending of humanity, but in a distinction of male and female. This initial identification is significant to recognise that male and female were being referred to as *both* reflecting the image of God, yet clearly in such a way that they were not identical, as they both needed and complemented each other. It was not that God just created a human; he created humans to be either male or female.

God continued and blessed the male and the female to "be fruitful and multiply. Fill the earth and govern it. Reign over the fish in the sea, the birds in the sky, and all the animals that scurry along the ground."[6] This verse is simple and familiar and can slip past us in its significance. However, we must pause and allow the truth of created order to influence us. The cultural mandate is being expressed as the creation covenant between God and humankind is established. This reveals both genders had been created, both commissioned to be fruitful, (for which they needed each other) and both were given the governing responsibilities over the created fish, birds and animals. At no point is superiority between the genders mentioned. There is, instead, complete equality. While there is a distinction established that merited the referencing of both male and female, there is no hierarchy established in creation based upon gender. As Groothuis and Peirce say, "biblical equality, therefore, denies that there is any created or otherwise God-ordained hierarchy based solely on gender."[7]

In response to God's creation, the final editor of Genesis keeps affirming that "God saw that it was good."[8] That is, until the creation of male and female. This pinnacle of creative mastery, said to be made in God's own image, was declared as "*very* good".[9]

We pause and allow the celebration of his creation to grip us. Let the party-poppers bang and the champagne corks fly! God was celebrating His creation and it was very good. Though we can never claim to have made a universe, we do all know what it is like to feel satisfied with what we have created. Cooking to feed the family is usually not a work of great creation, trying to get our five-a-day into a tasty menu. However, there are occasions when we love to cook. Some days the food served is just average, pleasant, edible, healthy and so on – but just *good*. The food produced for celebrations is different. Textures, tastes and temperature all combine to stimulate the senses so that you sit back from the meal knowing what you have eaten is *very good*. It is the banquets that we celebrate.

Or consider again the artist who paints still-life reflections. Some days you can gaze upon a picture and appreciate it as good and other times the brush strokes are so intricate and attentive that you find yourself wondering whether you are looking at a photograph rather than a painting. Some things are simply *very good*.

It is the creation of male *and* female, both distinct, (both reflecting God's image and both equal with no created hierarchy) that is celebrated by the creator as *very good*. Is it time we joined the celebrations and realised what is in fact, very good?

As God looked on that which he had created with pleasure and delight – since it was very good – surely we can celebrate the fact that diversity and difference co-existed between male and female, yet with no sense of subordination or domination. Biblical equality does not mean "sameness".

The creation story is a wonderful account of the master craftsman shaping and nurturing each animal and releasing them to "produce offspring of the same kind."[10] This then develops into God himself saying, "Let us create human beings in our image, to be like us."[11] Can you imagine the smile on his holy face as he moulded and crafted a representation and reflection of his perfection, wisdom, creativity, intelligence, beauty...?

Genesis continues with an exquisitely descriptive narrative of the garden with its flowing rivers and fruitful trees. Here we're introduced to the creation of humanity and to the idea that the male was created first, God forming him from mud and breathing life into his nostrils to create a "living person".[12] It was in this environment that the Lord gave some responsibility to the male to "tend and watch over it",[13] introducing the instruction that he was free to eat from any tree except the tree of the knowledge of good and evil.[14] What an incredible banquet-buffet. Notice, though, that the reader knows what the male has yet to figure out: the forbidden fruit will become a focus of desire.

The creation account we have in its current form combines the work of two authors, according to many scholars, redacted in antiquity to present us with chapter one and two. They provide two perspectives on what happened in Eden. In chapter one the animals are made first and then male and female created to rule over them. However, in chapter two it appears that male was made first, then the animals came as potential companions before him.

However, as Vallotton wrote in his book *Fashioned to Reign*, the created Adam would "not have been reproducing after their kind if they somehow procreated with the animals".[15] So it was for specific relational connectivity that God created the female. The creation of the female is said to be from the sleeping male's "side" where a rib was removed and remoulded. Vallotton explores the idea that the first human contained both male and female and did not become distinct until, "Adam was put to sleep, the Creator literally took the *she* out of the *he*. That means that the woman must have been *in* the man. Or God could not have taken her *out* of him."[16] This is an interesting thought suggesting that chapter one's humankind consisted of both male and female in the one created being and only separated into the two distinct humans in chapter two. Vallotton would suggest that "all the strengths of womanhood were removed from the man."[17] He is arguing for the completion of man being realised within marriage – the mystery of oneness. Men and women are incomplete without each other.[18]

We have two daughters. At different times they have both enjoyed seasons with best-friends. There was one time when one of them bought a friendship-necklace to share with her bestie. Have you seen them? Two necklaces with identical chains and a pendent hanging. But the pendent is in two halves. Each is able to "stand alone", but actually completes the friends' necklace pendant if they are put together.

The idea that men and women complete each other reinforces created equality. However, to us the main point to be drawn is that both male and female individually reflect the image of their creator, but when combined give a fuller and more complete reflection of the *imago Dei*. This unified reflection of God's nature is perhaps best seen in marriage, but should not be limited to matrimony. Whilst we can argue that male and female coming together in marriage is the pinnacle of God's self-revelation in human relationships, we believe there is much to be revealed of

God's glory and nature when this unity between the genders is seen outside the marital covenant. Whether married or single, we're created to reflect, in unified diversity, the synergy of divinity.

Male and female, we are created to be a true reflection, a very good reflection, of the very good nature of God. To be this very good reflection of the creator, we need male and female – not just in marriage, but in every aspect of life.

Chapter 4
Women: The last or the Least?

Let's stay with the order of creation a little longer. It crucially informs us when looking at the relationship between male and female, especially in the debate regarding inherent superiority. Who Comes First is a significant topic, and if misunderstood or mishandled can bring about more than a little tension. Ask any parent of twins! Or, consider a photo-finish of athletes where first equals best, faster or superior! Is order of overriding significance in all this?

If male was created first and female was created out of him then is there argument that she is less divinely created, less valuable and more subordinate? Vallotton's idea of the woman being contained already within the male suggests that she was there alongside male and it was in their separation that male and female were identified, then they were both, as if second! Humankind came first and male and female came second.

If however, the man was created first from mud and the woman was created from the side of the man then consider this: surely they were both really made from mud! It is apparent that both male and female were created by the same Creator and out of the same creative resource, mud, even though some would focus on the rib. Imagine a baker kneading a large batch of dough pulls some dough out to make a loaf of bread. Having shaped the bread and prepared it as complete the baker decides to make the loaf go further and wants to create another loaf. So the baker simply pulls some dough from the uncooked loaf and reforms it, producing two loaves. Is the second made of anything less than dough? Of course not, it was simply shaped from the pre-formed loaf instead of the original batch of dough! And, of course, with enough yeast and at the right temperature both loaves will rise and thrive and be deliciously-useful!

So could it be with male and female? The story begins that the male was made from mud. Later the Lord took some of that male-mud in the shape of rib and reformed a new creation, a female. Both made from the same supply and source. Both were crafted with the same love and attention and set for purpose. Both were created and looked upon as *very good*. One was not more 'very good' than the other.

From the detail of the creation of woman no announcement is made of authority or subordination. Instead, the writer draws straight into the revelation of unity saying 'the two are united into one'[19] in a sentence now used to understand marriage. There is no pre-fall authority outlined for the male only, arguably all that is explained is a sequence, a timeline of arrival. Last is not least, and first is not best.

The time line of arrival does not reveal any authority, value, or hierarchy. In fact sometimes it is quite the opposite.

If you have been to a traditional British wedding you might remember that after the ceremony the Bridal Party will stand in a receiving line to greet all their guests before the wedding breakfast is enjoyed. Then, once all the guests are in the venue, the bride and groom enter. They come in last because they are to be honoured. The Queen of England will be used to arriving last to a banquet not because she has run late and got caught in traffic on the way but because her arrival is held back to allow her to receive the honour she is due. Last does not mean least!

As the detail of the creation of male and female is established there is an emphasis on companionship made along with the statement made by God when he says 'It is not good for the man to be alone. I will make a helper who is just right for him'.[20]

A challenge of biblical interpretation means that there are often words we need to grapple with to be able to understand. Herein lies another tension in the understanding of what a *helper* is. Some would argue that a helper is a lowly position of subordination. A helper being less qualified, less experienced, carrying less authority and less significance within a situation, a bit like a learning-apprentice.

In their book on *The Message of Women,* Derek and Dianne Tidball encourage their readers to not misunderstand helper with any form of subordination as 'the helper assists others in the achievement of their task by lending strength to them in their weakness as, for example, when the word is used to describe one nation assisting another in warfare'[21] The majority of the time that the term 'helper' is used in the Old Testament it is in connection with describing God.

The Hebrew word for helper is *ezer,* and is used nineteen times in the Old testament, twice to describe a wife and seventeen times to describe God Himself.

Consider Psalm 146:5 'joyful are those who have the God of Israel as their helper' or Psalm 124:8 'Our help is from the Lord, who made heaven and earth'. Clearly God, as helper, is not subordinate to humankind, he does not have less authority, less wisdom, less experience, less knowledge or anything else. So in understanding the use of the language of the text as it was intended we can understand that, whilst identified as a helper the woman is not intentionally created to be subordinate to man. Instead she brings her unique gift, her own strengths and contribution.

While the language of helper is used to describe woman occasionally, and God often, we must not over-emphasise the comparison of the female helper as if she is like God as this could draw conclusions of superiority to the male and this pendulum-swing would be a corrective too far. However, it would be far more realistic to conclude that the female was neither subordinate nor superior but instead was created side-by-side, an equal human. The female was equal to the male, yet gloriously not the same.

The woman was created as neither last nor least.

Helen writes:

From the language of Genesis I might be Tim's primary 'ezer' but that doesn't limit my gift from also bringing strength to other relationships with both males and females. My leadership gift is not because I am married whilst it does get expressed within my marriage.

When we stepped into church leadership it became apparent that it would be beneficial for our church family for Tim to gain accreditation as a minister within our denomination. Again, it was not something that I even considered at that stage. However, well over ten years later I wanted to do further theological studies to help me grow both personally but also in my preaching and communication. I was advised that ministerial accreditation would be a positive theological training to pursue. There was also a recognition between us that the more I grow the more I could help others grow, and this would be important for both men and women.

As part of my ministerial accreditation application I needed to get a personal reference which would normally be done by a church leader. In my case it seemed inappropriate to get Tim to do this so I approached another leader. I chose someone who knew me well, loved me and had observed my ministry, and had heard my preaching. Following my request I was asked to meet with my referee and was greeted by a surprising statement with words along the line of "Helen, I can't support your application because if we do this for you what would we do with all the other wives? What if they all want to be ministers?"

The shock of this statement stole my voice, my courage and any fight that was left in me. If this is what represented the denomination that I was applying to be a minister of then I was not going to be able to represent it well. I pressed an instant 'pause' on my application and simply got on with leading where I was welcome. I didn't need a title to lead locally – so whilst restricted I was not completely shackled.

Leaders are not made because they are married as this would prohibit the plethora of very gifted, able leaders who happen to be single. Yet equally leaders should not be restricted because they are married.

It was nearly a year later before I would even reconsider entering again the process of ministerial accreditation. One of the national leaders at the time was an Australian fireball by the name of Gary Rucci. He absolutely understood that gift was not gender affirmed or limited and he asked me, for the sake of the next generation of women leaders, to press through the process and reapply. This time Gary put his name to my application and helped me to refine my voice and courage by giving me his. Because of Gary's partnership and his recognition of what God had placed in me, and wanted to do through me, I was no longer overlooked.

So a picture has been sketched in this chapter of a glorious Eden – a garden ripe with fruit and green with perfection and Adam and Eve sharing equality, clothed in dignity and reflecting in their difference as well as in their similarities, the glory of God. Then, the war began. Next we'll look at where it all went south.

Chapter 5
It began to go horribly wrong

We've been considering where this fight between us began and with Genesis as our inspiration, we see the story played out in front of a backdrop of beauty; a faultless garden. It is hard to imagine the beauty and dignity of that pre-war peace. Before sin entered the scene, before we started fighting each other. What was it like when male and female were content and complete with each other, in relationship with God? They knew what it was like to walk with God in the cool of the day, without any sorrow, pain, fear, doubt or surrounding troubles. Everything was going so well when from stage left came the serpent.

Here comes the devil, our now-familiar enemy, tempting and taunting and casting doubt on what God had previously said. Eve and Adam, as they were now called, were in the garden together and although Eve is the one recorded talking with the serpent and eating the fruit first, Adam "who was with her"[22] also took and ate the fruit when the invitation was extended to him.

The Genesis narrative does not identify the serpent as the devil. The serpent was seen in antiquity as the enemy of God's creation, and as this story was told over the generations the serpent became synonymous with Satan, the accuser. If we are going to understand what biblical equality is really all about and that we have a common enemy, it begins with the acknowledgement that the biblical framework for the fall is the presence of a very real, personal enemy who was in the paradise of Eden.

In the story, the enemy sows the idea of the forbidden fruit being more delicious than dangerous, by twisting God's word. The fruit is consumed. Oh, how often a sinful choice can taste delicious at the outset! We read here what most of us have experienced at some time if we're honest. The initial pleasure of selfish indulgence suddenly twists into the devastation of consequence. Adam and Eve were probably still dribbling fruit-juice down their chins, licking their sticky fingers, when reality dawned. See their response. The immediate result of the consumption of the forbidden fruit was that "at that moment their eyes were opened and they suddenly felt shame at their nakedness. So they sewed fig leaves together to cover themselves."[23] Like the optician who shines a bright torch into his patient's eyes to see if their pupils contract, the first humans' reaction to the consequence of their choice is automatic. Their eyes are suddenly opened; they cannot keep them closed. Shame gripped them with an intensity that compelled and repelled them to retreat and hide. Their nakedness was revealed and shame moved into their hearts and began to divide their home.

The text does not say specifically what part of their bodies they covered up and so caution must be applied. However, scholars generally agree the text implies they did not cover up their knees or their elbows, or their embarrassing feet. They did not cover up their eyes that had gazed upon the fruit, nor the hands that had reached out and touched it. They did not cover their mouths that had tasted the fruit. Instead, it is widely agreed they covered up their genitalia.

The part of their bodies that Adam and Eve covered in response to their sin and shame were the very parts that made them distinctly male and female. Sin and shame enters and the relationship between male and female powerfully diminishes their differences and, as result, highlights their similarities. Whilst there is much more to distinguish male and female than their physical anatomy, the uniqueness that was celebrated before in their maleness and femaleness is suddenly covered up. Their distinctives are covered. The simple trust and innocence of their naked differences is replaced by a lifelong longing to make or find their own dignity. They are now weighed down by shame and it will become a wedge between them. So Adam and Eve cover their uniqueness and leave on show that which is the same between them.

Understanding equality requires grappling with the implications of how sameness and diversity are to be reflected in human community, and how all that works in relationship to our dependence on God. Let's look at this briefly. The ultimate power-grab took place by that fruit tree. Adam and Eve grasped for independence, so that they would no longer be dependent on their Creator. What's more they wouldn't be dependent on each other. Instead of needing each other, or God, they started a path of self-rule and independence. By covering their nakedness perhaps they were covering those differences that reminded them of their need for each other? They are independent of God and now each other, and the result is that they now look the same.

We see here some dangers to avoid and an opportunity. Are the differences between male and female significant to understanding ourselves, our value and significance, and therefore something to be reclaimed? There is a risk that our pursuit of sameness and independence from each other works against our God-given mandate to celebrate diversity between male and female, even rejoicing in our need for each other. We mustn't over-compensate *or* over-emphasise the differences. We need wisdom here. We do recognise scientifically-proven genetic differences in male and female physiology, and also accept that in general terms this includes variance in typical male and female psychology and therefore behaviour. Even on a cellular level, there is a chromosomal variation between men and women. As a result, there are some traits that have been proven to span cultures and are not therefore merely a product of nurture. God-given nature is at work. However, we must be careful to not play into the enemy's hands. Way too easily gender stereotyping is used to restrict males and females to certain tasks and roles, and put them under limits that are not designed by God. We construct ungodly limitations. As we explore gender roles in the Church and wider society, we need to keep this tension in mind as Jenny Baker warns in her book *Equals*: "Over-focusing on difference can be an excuse for laziness and a way of justifying immature behaviour instead of doing the work of growing up."[24]

We will come back to this later. In the meantime, let's return to Adam and Eve's predicament in the Garden.

The two first humans were gripped by shame and longed to hide away. They were no longer at peace with each other as they squirmed and blame-shifted. They covered their uniqueness and no longer felt able to walk freely in the garden nor fellowship openly with the Lord. Paradise was lost and the great division had begun. Peace had been broken and the war began. As we have mentioned, because of the fall, man and woman now seek greater similarity, long for peaceful equality and hide their genitals. They cover up their distinctives. Now, before you get inspired to throw caution to the wind and start removing clothing in order to prove a certain level of freedom and dignified equality with the world, let's move on! We're exploring the connection between our gender identities, shame, and where the battle of the sexes began.

It was the Lord's compassionate response to Adam and Eve that he "made clothing from animal skins for Adam and his wife."[25] Imagine their gratitude as the Lord stooped to their level and lovingly covered their shame, feeling their pain, helplessness and deep regret. Consider how the Lord took another of his creatures and prepared the skin to cover them. His mercy and kindness never ceases to amaze! God fashions garments to restore their physical dignity. He longed to make that which was once *very good* to be *very good again*. Consider Adam and Eve's relief and gratitude. Imagine their tears of penitence, rolling down their reddened cheeks, mixing with the sticky fruit-juice, washing their faces. They wiped sorrow from their faces with sweetened fingers fresh from sin. Also, imagine God's tears rolling with regret for what had happened. His fingers moved to make the covering by which their shame would be clothed. Where Adam and Eve reacted to try and cover their sin, the Lord desired redemption and clothed them.

Wouldn't Adam and Eve's hearts have burst with the combined awareness of their own sin and their gratitude for the garments of grace much like Isaiah, when he cried out, "I am overwhelmed with joy in the Lord my God! For he has dressed me with the clothing of salvation and draped me in a robe of righteousness."[26]

Has not the Lord continued to stoop to the level of humanity and made it possible for sin to be covered?

The garments were not the only things though, that Adam and Eve came away with. First there was a significant one-sided discourse from the Creator to the fallen created. The implications of their actions were spelled out and the consequences for their choices became apparent. That's where we go next – to the conversation that followed the fall in Genesis chapter 3.

CHAPTER 6
3:16

The battle of the sexes has been raging for a long, long time, and as with any argument it is important to recognise where it all began. Like any argument with children, perhaps, one of the things that matters is "who started it". Get to that point and justice is easier to find. We're looking at where the fight between men and women began and the consequences of Adam and Eve's sin on how we all relate together. Ancient covenants always have an element of condition to them, including a "curse" if the covenant is broken. Depending on the nature of the deity, the idea of a curse carries different connotations. For the loving and equally just Creator of the Bible, we see that a curse in his terms was an avoidable consequence of breaking the agreement. It is not to be seen as a spiritual spell cast by a hateful Almighty, but the love-filled explanation of what rebellion and disobedience will lead to.

Here in Genesis, then, we can say it started with a curse.

The Lord addresses the serpent first, so we will start here. The serpent becomes cursed and legless as he crawls around in the dust. Notice that the serpent is cursed to grovel in the dust, but some translations say, "you will eat dust all the days of your life."[27] This is an important point; hold it in your mind for a little bit as we will be coming back to this.

The curse unfolds further to show that there will be a specific hatred between the serpent and the woman. The particular animosity between Satan and women is really significant to our understanding of biblical equality and the dangers of friendly fire. While the enemy is also seeking the destruction of men, as the offspring of the woman in the future would be both male and female, there is clearly a particular animosity regarding this first woman, Eve. This has led some to conclude that the enemy has a particular animosity towards all women, carriers of all future offspring. Vallotton observes this as a reason for societal inequality as "the devil hates women even more than he hates men... therefore; demonic warfare is more often focused against women."[28] This is such a significant point to grasp. The enemy holds particular animosity towards women! His strategy is targeted against women. We see signs of this all over our world and even closer to home. If this is a specific strategy of the enemy we must surely be cautious and open to admit the dangers if we intentionally or even inadvertently join the wrong side of the battlefield.

If this truth of the enemy's heightened animosity towards women does not profoundly impact you, then reconsider the global evidence for the persecution, oppression and restriction of women.

Tim writes:

A thought specifically for all those men reading this book: I reckon we need to calmly and honestly face up to some of the challenges explored here about how we have treated women. Look at evil regimes around the world and sadly you will see men dominating, oppressing, limiting and diminishing women. This takes the form of violent pornography (or, frankly, pornography of pretty much any sort) which objectifies women for our own satisfaction, prostitution, female genital mutilation and a thousand other atrocious acts of wilful harm. As well as these more obvious atrocities, sometimes our mistreatment of women is more subtle and harder to pinpoint. Like how women are treated in workplaces, the education system, in government. I for one recognise my own culpability and the heartfelt desire for the Kingdom of God to reign in my life and in our church, town and the nations, where men and women are free to be who God intended us to be. This is a crucial part of our exploration in this book, where we are recognising the need to stop fighting each other and instead fight together.

Continuing through the curse there is further implication between the serpent and the woman as a generational battle is launched offspring-to-offspring. Whilst the serpent is not named as the devil, it is widely understood that he represents the accuser, Satan. From paradise to peril, the children of God were faced with God's arch enemy and his people entered into an inter-generational battle. It is this desire to rob the next generation of its very life which is a stronghold of the enemy; one we should wake up to quickly.

Is it because every human on the planet has come from the womb of a woman that the enemy particularly hates women and their offspring? Perhaps. Let's not forget, though, that every baby in a woman's womb needed a man to be involved too! Is it because one day a woman would carry a baby in her womb that did not get there with man's involvement? For Mary, "while she was still a virgin, she became pregnant through the power of the Holy Spirit."[29] Did the enemy of God have a sense of what was to come? We're not sure. The enemy is not omniscient or all-knowing. However, there are other times we read of the enemy of God killing many children in order to destroy just one. Consider the time when Mary and Joseph had to flee with the infant Jesus to avoid the killing of all children under the age of two years at the hand of Herod's soldiers. Could it be that the devil would target all women just in case there was produced from her womb a child of significance?

This targeting of women and the intention to fight against the next generation is a strategically important truth for us to grasp in our stand for ending friendly fire. We must recognise the real enemy.

The final implications of the curse for the devil are in what can be described as the "head" and "heel" implications. The woman's offspring would crush the head of the snake, while he would strike at their heel. The enemy's desire is to prohibit humans from walking with God. Adam and Eve had loved walking in the Garden of Eden with the Lord and the first thing that happened when their shame was realised was that they hid and did not walk in the Garden. This is why the Lord had to "call" for them. It is walking with the Lord that was impacted.

Helen writes:

A few years ago I was training to run a half-marathon with my sister. All was going really well and I was loving the training, grabbing regular chances for shorter runs each week and setting out once a week on a longer run. I use the term "run" with caution, technically it was more of a jog! Running ten miles was a pleasurable experience to me, but a friend of mine could run a full marathon in the same time! Nonetheless, I was moving at a speed faster than a walk and enjoying it. Two weeks before the race things quite literally turned on the heel, my heel! My Achilles tendon became inflamed and put an end to the race. I now have a new sympathy for the people of Galatia when Paul wrote to them saying, "you were running the race so well, who has held you back from following the truth?"[30] With an injury grabbing at my heel I was unable to run. Back in the garden the consequences of their actions meant that Eve and her offspring were going to have an enemy constantly trying to grab at their heels, trying to trip them, bite them, injure them and stop them from moving forward.

Are we the sons and daughters of Eve's offspring?

Although the serpent would attack the heel, the woman's offspring would attack the enemy's head. Why? It is the head that represents the area of thinking, of strategy and decision. If we can recognise the enemy's strategies for what they are, then we can win the battle and remain walking with the Lord.

Consider the prophecy of Hosea: "Let those who are wise understand these things. Let those with discernment listen carefully. The paths of the Lord are true and right, and righteous people live by walking in them. But in those paths sinners stumble and fall."[31]

It is so important that our walk with the Lord is not impacted by the enemy's strategy for our destruction.

The Lord turns to Eve next with the implications of her actions as the consequence in the curse are exposed. Again the implications linked with the next generation are apparent. The initial consequence is linked to childbirth with pain being increased in the delivery of children. The implication is that birth had always involved pain, and that pain is being increased, rather than introduced. Perhaps not all pain is bad, as this suggests that a form of pain before the curse was by divine design and not as a consequence of sin. Maybe the Lord wanted to limit the number of people born in the future, knowing that painful activities are not always desired to be repeated?! As parents of three, however, we can affirm that there is a gift of amnesia, brought about by a chemical involuntary response, which means that in spite of the pain of delivery, it is a process women go through repeatedly and usually willingly for the sake of the outcome.

Perhaps there is another significant reason why the pain of childbirth is allowed to increase. Giving birth requires huge strength from women and it can feel like a battle is taking place in their bodies. The war the enemy was going to wage against the next generation would initially be fought by parents, in particular the mother, to protect the child. It is as if the Lord is enabling and empowering women to take their ground and be willing to fight for their child, right at the start.

Helen writes:

I have been blessed by the privilege of having three babies. At one point during the birth of my first child I was holding Tim's hand. I promise I wasn't trying to hurt him, nor was I intentionally wanting to show him what pain was really like, but I did nearly break his digits! Years later when I had our second child, I determined not to actually hold his hand at all. Instead, in somewhat of a weird straddling posture (don't picture it!) I was holding the side of the bed. At one point, apparently (I was too focused to care) it took all of Tim's and the midwife's collective strength to pull in the opposite direction of my leverage, so that the bed didn't collapse on top of me! I don't understand it, but I was powerful in that moment! The strength of a woman in labour is a strength that is going to be needed in later battles. We have it within us, more than we know!

The next sentence of the curse is perhaps the most revealing when deciphering the enemy's strategy to get us fighting each other. God says to Eve in Genesis 3:16, "you will desire to control your husband, but he will rule over you."[32] Here it is spelled out, crystal clear and plain to see. The desire of Eve to control Adam was an outworking of her new-found independence from God and from him. Furthermore, the apparent result was that Adam would independently rule over Eve and overpower her. Control and rule is hereby introduced into the relationship which had previously been established in equity and co-dependence on their Creator. Adam and Eve reached for a forbidden fruit and that one action resulted in a gender battle pursuing control and rule over each other. This is war.

This was not God's design. He created men and women to enjoy shared dominion, to live and steward creation together. To share leadership, if you like. This independent urge to self-rule led to a determination to control and dominate others. Such were (and are) the devastating consequence of selfish sin and the rejection of God's sovereignty over us. Here in 3:16 we see equality and unity between male and female disappearing with a bite from the fruit of good and evil.

The implications of the curse regarding men come into perspective with Eve as we've just seen. However, then the Lord turns his full attention onto Adam. It becomes apparent that the responsibility to working in the garden has gone from a gentle *tend-and-watch* to *sweat-and-scratch* living. Just as pregnancy and childbirth become more painful for the woman, work becomes harder for the man – both consequences directly impacting the command for them to *be fruitful*. If it is hard to do something, we instinctively avoid it, don't we? We look for the easiest route, for time- and effort-saving devices. Furthermore, if something is painful, it is often not repeated. We look for a more comfortable way. When the war began, Adam was cursed with the reality that any fruitfulness was going to come from *hard work*.

Adam was going to have to prove himself to be able to turn his labour into a harvest. Many psychologists would conclude that men have an especially deep longing to be respected; respected for what they do and what they achieve. Of course, any demand for respect is matched by the reality that respect has to be earned. This fallen, broken desire for respect is an expression of the hard labour of achievement expressed in this curse. Here at the start of the fight, men are destined to have to work hard for any outcomes. Nothing is going to come easy. Everything will have to be worked for, to be earned.

The curse concludes with the reality spoken to Adam that by the "sweat of your brow will you have food to eat until you return to the ground from which you were made. For you were made from dust, and to dust you will return."[33]

Now remember that earlier thought. A few paragraphs ago we looked at the curse directed at the serpent. The serpent was told that he would eat dust and now Adam is being told that he will return to dust. In other words, Adam's choice to disobey God and sin was going to result in him returning to the ground from which he was formed. Not only that, in doing so he was going to become snake-food! As a consequence of sin and the curse, Adam would end up being consumed by the enemy.

This is not a condition that the Lord wanted to leave Adam in, nor is it a consequence that anyone of us would want to be left in. The curse is not how we are to live. We are not meant to be consumed by the enemy. As we consider these things, let this over-familiar text re-grip your heart. The enemy was going to be snapping at the heel, trying to trip and defeat the offspring from walking with the Lord. The enemy, whilst restricted to ground level, was going to be eating the dust of our offspring.

Friends of God, hear the warning, see the strategy. Allow the fog of war to lift and see what the enemy (as a consequence of our sin) is getting up to. Hell is let loose among us and especially between us. We have turned against each other, seen each other as the enemy.

We want to share with you some insight from powerful partnerships in the Bible which show the power of facing our common enemy. Before we do that, we'll take another look at the curse and its consequences in our relationships as male and female in light of some teaching from the New Testament. The curse has been reversed.

CHAPTER 7
THE CURSE – LIVING WITH THE CONSEQUENCES

So we recognise that this curse, the consequence of Adam and Eve's sin, had massive ramifications for women, for men, and for our relationships with each other, as well as our work and child-bearing. War was declared and our enemy turned us against each other.

The Apostle Paul had a lot to say about the implications of the fall. Writing to the church in Ephesus, he urged them to be aware of the battle that they were in as believers. Not a physical war with human enemies, but a war that was far more sinister. A battle that was against "the evil rulers and authorities of the unseen world, against mighty powers in this dark world, and against evil spirits in the heavenly places."[34]

Paul is not like a scare-monger who just writes about fear and impending doom. Paul writes with a father's heart. He writes not in fear but in love for the children of God, for the early believers, for those whose heart is open to God and listening to the voice of the Spirit. We thank God that this letter has survived the test of time and is preserved for us. Paul not only tells them, and us, about the dangers and inevitability of war, he explains how to survive and thrive in the context of a war in the heavenly realms.[35]

"Put on all of God's armour so that you will be able to stand firm against all strategies of the devil."[36]

For those who were blessed to have been introduced to Jesus at an early age you might have gone to a Sunday school class. If so, we imagine that in your memory bank will be pictures of Paul's armour and what each piece represents. Our spiritual armour is incredibly significant and essential in understanding and standing against the enemy's strategies.

Do you remember the story of Nehemiah when he took on the challenge, at the Lord's invitation, to rebuild the city walls of Jerusalem? He was so aware of the physical battle that he entered when taking on this labour that he lived permanently ready for work and war. He never took his kit off! He never put down his sword.[37] This is what we need to be like.

A phrase Helen likes to use amongst family, colleagues and friends is that it is good to "live ready". For Tim, it is usually in a sporting context urging team members to be "on the front foot". Sluggish competitors lose the game and sleepy soldiers lose their lives and endanger the lives of others.

The great wall-restoring Nehemiah was one leader who was always living ready. Paul was urging the Ephesians to do the same. If we want to be strong in the Lord and stand undefeated in life's battle we will be someone who lives ready, too!

The best soldiers know how to fight as a team. They need to be aware of their own strengths, capabilities and strategies along with an awareness of the strength, capabilities and strategies of their enemies. Confidence and certainty can give way to confusion very quickly in war environments. No wonder Paul reminds the Ephesian believers that the mind must be protected by the helmet at all times and that all their kit is held together by the belt of truth.

Adam and Eve begin to kick up the dust around them and in doing so are not recognising who the real enemy is. We see in Genesis that Adam immediately tries to identify Eve as the one responsible for the catastrophe, while she diverts the blame to the snake. No one wants to take responsibility and division is the result.

The essence of this book, though, is that there is power in the Christian faith, essentially in the work of the cross of Jesus and the power of his Holy Spirit that brings ultimate victory. The antidote to the curse in Genesis 3:16 is the grace confirmed in John 3:16. Namely, "for God loved the world so much that he gave his one and only Son, so that everyone who believes in him will not perish but have everlasting life."

Think about it: Do we not celebrate the hope we have in Christ at the funeral of a believer, when we say that they are not limited to being in the dust and consumed by the enemy, because they will rise and be with Christ for eternity?[38] Do we not anticipate that God has brought salvation to earth through Christ; that truly believing in him sets us free from the enemy's grip? Surely then we should not be selective in our understanding of the implications of the truth in John 3:16, and instead let that truth infiltrate the burden of Genesis 3:16. We need to recognise that the real enemy to equality is not that we fight each other under the curse, but that we fail to fight together in the light of the cross. Instead, we can choose to rise up, side-by-side in God-restored equality, and rule together as men and women, fighting the *real* enemy.

When men and women are truly following Jesus, changed by him, serving him, the relationships we have with each other will be transformed. That is God's plan. No one needs remain victim to the consequences of the curse because we can live in the consequences of the cross. Wonderful news! It is through the gift of grace and mercy in Christ that "to all who believed him and accepted him, he gave the right to become children of God. They are reborn—not with a physical birth resulting from human passion or plan, but a birth that comes from God."[39] Salvation is available to all through the re-birth in Christ.

Remember that the strategy for bringing clarity to the "fog of war" is *to feel out the truth with the measure of its judgment.* Now that the fog is lifting a little, perhaps we can see the real enemy who has been in our garden all along. Perhaps we can see the enemy skulking around the edges of the paradise we thought we were enjoying. As cunning as our enemy is, he is prone to repeat his strategies, like a General with limited tactics. All too often the enemy of the Lord comes alongside people like you and us and engages us in a conversation which starts with the question, "Did God say?" With these three words he sows doubt and suggests compromise.

"Did God say?"

With these three words he seeks to bite the heel and hinder our walk. With these three words he seeks to trip up and destroy this generation and prevent the next generation from existence.

But let's remember, Christians, we have been set free from the curse through the cross. We have been rescued from being consumed by the enemy through Christ's death and resurrection. Remember when Jesus was baptised by his cousin John, the Holy Spirit descended upon him like a dove and the audible voice of the Father was heard reaffirming his love for His beloved son. Straight after this wonderful encounter the Holy Spirit led him into the wilderness, where He was tested and proven to be all that God said he was. Much like in the Garden of Eden, the enemy came alongside Jesus speaking doubt and asking him, "*If* you are the son of God...." Just as he asked Eve, "*Did* God say...." Yet Jesus did not make this an opportunity for a conversation. Instead he stamped truth with a strong answer: "It is written..." Jesus knew the scriptures well and recognised the weapon that they are. He wielded this weapon and swiftly dealt with every word-dart the enemy threw.

Surely this is something we can learn from Jesus when facing the darts the enemy throws, as he seeks to wreak havoc with our relationships.

So when the enemy asks, "Did God say that he wanted women to desire to control their husbands, and men to rule over women?" we can simply and confidently answer, "It is written..."

"So God created human beings in his own image. In the image of God he created them; male and female he created them. Then God blessed them and said, 'Be fruitful and multiply. Fill the earth and govern it. Reign over the fish in the sea, the birds in the sky, and all the animals that scurry along the ground.' Then God said, 'Look! I have given you every seed-bearing plant throughout the earth and all the fruit trees for your food. And I have given every green plant as food for all the wild animals, the birds in the sky, and the small animals that scurry along the ground—everything that has life.' And that is what happened. Then God looked over all he had made, and he saw that it was very good!"[40]

Let us celebrate that which is *very good*. Let us celebrate the intended created equality. Let us stop fighting for control amongst ourselves and fight our enemy together. The work of Jesus on the cross was a complete work, and it has been the testimony of the Church ever since he rose from the dead and sent his Holy Spirit, that we can and should and will live the life of heaven's kingdom here on this earth. And in the kingdom of heaven there is no in-fighting, no shame, and men and women serve together with dignity, honour and strength.

This is not a pipe-dream of impossibility, or just something we wait to enjoy in heaven. It can be our reality today.

So, we've established where the war began and how our fighting each other started with our sin and a curse. But in Christ we know

NO MORE FRIENDLY FIRE

that curse has been reversed. In the next section we're going to look at four biblical partnerships between male and female that have been gloriously redeemed. They demonstrate how we can live today in light of their example. Read on – there is so much more to share!

Implications and application – some questions

- Why do you think Christian men and women, even with what is known and experienced of the cross of Christ and his grace, still struggle to avoid living under the curse placed on Adam and Eve?
- What would it look and feel like to be in a Church where the male/female battle was truly over and healing was experienced and lived out in daily reality? How different would this be?
- How could the Church impact wider society if we lived in light of the "curse reversed"? What would we have to demonstrate to those around us?
- How would you suggest influencers and leaders in your part of the Church respond to this? What should they say or do to move us in the right direction?

A prayer

Loving Father, we know our sin was and is ugly. It pushes us away from you and from each other. Forgive us for our selfish ways.

Lord Jesus, thank you for your restoring work on the cross, where you bring us together as equals and present us – male and female – as equally forgiven and accepted around your Father's table. Thank you for your grace!

Holy Spirit, I know you are the Spirit of unity. I ask you to change me, and change us all in your Church, so we might experience more fully the blessings that come with your work in our lives when we end our wars with each other and fight the powers of darkness together.

Unite us again, more deeply. In Jesus' name,

Amen.

Section 3: Shoulder to Shoulder

In this section we are going to be looking at four inspirational examples of men and women who fought together; not each other, *together* – against the enemy who inspires evil kings, corrupt rulers, social injustice and faithless idolatry.

These men and women were not all married, not all the same age and not even from the same tribes, but their shining example from the pages of Scripture compels us to consider again what it means for men and women to fight for God's kingdom shoulder-to-shoulder.

As you read their stories again, or even for the first time, be prepared to see how God uses men and women in different ways, with different roles that are unique to each occasion, to further his glorious purposes. They were used according to their gift and not because of their gender to bring hope and freedom to this world. To put the enemy in his place and to push back the kingdom of darkness. Here's to the ones who won the war and inspire us to do the same.

CHAPTER 8
SWEETNESS, LIGHTNING AND A TORCH

Helen writes:

In 2014 a prophetic church leader from Asia was over in England. Tim and I went to hear him doing a seminar on church leadership and then were blessed when he prayed for all the delegates and prophesied over us. Part of what he prayed over me was that I was a daughter of Deborah. In earthly terms I'm the daughter of an amazing woman of faith called Valerie… but he wasn't talking biologically! For a long time, not that he knew this, I've held Deborah in high esteem. She has truly been a hero to me. So can you imagine my heart-racing delight to have heard her name in a prophetic prayer over me.

While we are arguably all sons and daughters of Adam and Eve, we also need some of the DNA from Deborah and the leading-man in her story, Barak. Watch how they fight together…

In a male-dominated culture the story of Deborah makes an interesting read. Her name means "bee"[41] and the sweetness of Deborah to her friends, contrasted with the sting she gave to her enemies, is linguistically exquisite! Deborah, a mother to Israel and a godly woman, is first introduced to readers acting as a judge and prophet to Israel. Prophets rose up time and again when God's people were oppressed or in trouble. Sometimes this trouble came as a result of the people's sins, idol worship and corruption, and the prophets were sent with strong warnings to urge repentance. Other times the prophets came to warn against and provide strategy for fighting their military or social oppressors. Deborah comes to notoriety operating as a prophet at a time when the Israelites were being oppressed by their enemy, Jabin.[42]

It's so wonderful when God speaks personally and profoundly to people at just the right time. There are painful times when he is silent, and we have to wait and trust. There are other times, however, when we are ready to quit, give up, despair or turn the wrong way, that the voice of the Lord speaks. Boom! In those moments we just need to be willing to listen and then, of course, obey. This story is about one of those moments.

Deborah was clearly an anointed woman who held the office of a prophet. She was reputed to both hear God's voice and do his will. These are important qualities to acknowledge and emulate if we want to glean all the truth and apply it. Being a hearer of God's will is not enough. The response to put it into action is the next essential step. Reading books, even the Bible, is not enough; we have to learn from the truth and allow it to become our practice rather than simply our principle. Deborah was respected by her peers and her wisdom was sought because people could see she was empowered by God. Observe that the people of the day were prepared to acknowledge the anointing, and to seek the counsel of a woman. The message was desired more than the gender of the messenger. Deborah did not shy away from exerting her authority or acting on what she received from the Lord. She did not hide behind her gender or question the Lord's choice of using her as a prophet. She simply heard and acted upon what the Lord told her.

So one day Deborah hears from the Lord and immediately summons Barak to her counsel, to give the Lord's word to him. Here's an extract of the story from Judges 4 as we hear Deborah sharing an oracle with Barak:

"This is what the Lord, the God of Israel, commands you: 'Call out 10,000 warriors from the tribes of Naphtali and Zebulun at Mount Tabor. And I will call out Sisera, commander of Jabin's army, along with his chariots and warriors, to the Kishon River. There I will give you victory over him.'

Barak told her, 'I will go, but only if you go with me.'

'Very well,' she replied, "I will go with you. But you will receive no honour in this venture, for the Lord's victory over Sisera will be at the hands of a woman.'" So Deborah went with Barak to Kedesh. At Kedesh, Barak called together the tribes of Zebulun and Naphtali, and 10,000 warriors went up with him. Deborah also went with him."[43]

Barak was a Hebrew warrior who led the army. His name is said to mean "lightning"[44] and he did not hesitate to honour Deborah's invitation to meet. Barak was not too proud to hear the wisdom of the prophet and submit to listening and acting upon what she said. He listened to Deborah as she gave specific, strategic instructions to him for the raising of an army. Whilst Deborah had no ambitions to lead the army herself she was given the divine authority and human respect to raise someone who could. So she instructed the reputed military leader, Barak of Naphtali, to lead the crusade. Deborah the prophet is instructing Barak the army leader by giving him the strategies for success in battle. But the advice is not limited to simply commanding from afar.

Barak was willing to go, to be obedient to the Lord's instruction through her, but only on condition that she went too. Barak may have had the strength to lead the army, but he seemed to lack the wisdom and discernment of God's voice to do so victoriously. Barak is not satisfied to simply take the advice of the mother-of-Israel, the prophet Deborah. He is not satisfied just holding court with her and receiving strategy. He wants her to go on the mission with him. The anointing that is on her by the Lord himself is what Barak wants to keep close to him and his warriors on the battlefield. He wants to win for God and knows that unity with Deborah is a powerful weapon. Barak does not want to go to battle unless Deborah is nearby him, offering constant counsel and being a direct channel to the Lord. Taking her with him will perhaps symbolically confirm that he is also taking God with him. Barak does not want to embark on this military mission without Deborah's active involvement, nor the Lord's.

Isn't it fascinating that Barak does not raise the issue of gender? Deborah is clearly very aware of the implications of Barak's request for her participation. She warns Barak that his previous and positive reputation will not grow if she is with him, because it means that the victory will be seen as involving the leading presence of a woman. Yet, he does not back down in his insistence that Deborah go with him. Barak values the presence of the Lord, the opportunity to hear instruction from the him, and the success of his mission more than he values his own reputation. He is willing to acknowledge weakness for the sake of victory.

Barak's response is very important in our understanding today if we are going to live with restored relationships. Our modern trend to embrace celebrity culture, grow our digital influence and increase our followers is all about making a name for ourselves. Our desire for self-expression and obsession with presenting a positive image is challenged by Barak's behaviour. He was not concerned about his reputation. He was willing to risk some of his credibility as a warrior by aligning with a woman.

It is time we became those courageous leaders in the Church who will raise a generation of similar men and women, who will consider the outcome more important than their personal reputations. We need to release warriors who will recognise that the real enemy can be overcome when we align men and women together, according to gift and anointing. This is a victory in itself, for sure, and we can see that releasing women into their areas of gift requires stronger men, not weaker ones. Barak, you hero! You acknowledged that you couldn't fight, or lead, alone.

Some might argue that Barak's insistence on Deborah's involvement shows his lack of confidence. We're not so sure. We see this as a confident man recognising his need of help. It is a bold man who enlists the help of a woman, heeds her advice, submits to her gift, and responds to what she brings when anointed by the Lord. Just as the Lord assigned Eve to come as the helper to Adam, so Deborah comes as the expert to bring strength, anointing and ultimately victory to Barak.

Similarly, Deborah values the success of the mission and obedience to the Lord's word more than she values her own safety. Here is a man and a woman of boldness. He would not go without her wisdom and she was willing to be in the grunting, blood-soaked male-terrain of battle for the sake of God's victory. Deborah did not shy away from the dangers of combat. Instead, she stood confidently in the purposes of God and of the anointing she knew had been given by him. Significantly, she did not fall into the trap of the curse and seek to control Barak. She advised him and outlined strategy, but was not insistent that she had to be there to make sure all went well. She's not pushing for control, just playing her part. She's not insisting on being there, but Barak invites her. Notice that neither Deborah nor Barak fell into the trap of the curse. In their symbiotic relationship they were able to deliver the Israelites from the hands of their oppressors. Their greatest gifts shone not in self-sufficiency, but synchronicity. It is this side-by-side synergy that enabled God's strategy to unfold.

Read the rest of the blood-stained chapter of Judges and you will see how it all works out. It is not for the faint-hearted, as war rages and a now-infamous tent peg pierces the enemy's skull in the hands of Jael, a cunning woman warrior.

Step back from this story and you will see the power of Deborah and Barak fighting the enemy of God's people together, each operating in their area of strength. This is the coming together of a male and female leader to fight a real enemy together and to lead the Israelites into victory in battle. Both were leaders of different gifting who became a powerful combination when released to be leaders in their own way, together. Each of them made space for the other's gifts and each of them offered their own gifts to be used in the mission. It was this sacrificial-generosity that enabled the victory to be won.

At no point in this biblical story does the author cast doubt on Deborah's God-given appointment as prophet to Israel, or in her ability and validity as a leader. Nor does the leader revel in the loss of reputation that Barak risks with the recruitment of a woman to his team. It simply shows that their relationship is part of the prophetic call to the Israelites at the time. The story recalls Deborah's position in authority much as it does some of the other judges who served Israel in season. Deborah, a woman, was released to be a leader of a nation, teaching, advising, instructing and going to battle.

In the spiritual battles which we face today, whose advice are we willing to seek? Who do we go to asking for their involvement? Does our pride rob us of forging winning partnerships?

Whilst Deborah was not looking for involvement in the army, she did not shy away from it. Her motivation was to ensure that she was faithful to dispatch the word of God that was revealed to her. Have you ever experienced one of those times when we become the answer to our own prayers and the solution to our own challenges? On this occasion, Deborah became not only the voice that God chose to speak through, but the means by which he brought about victory for the people of Israel.

Had Deborah not gone into that battle then the war against the Canaanite king Jabin would perhaps have been lost. Sometimes obedience to the purposes of the Lord requires us to trust his protection over others better than our ability to protect them ourselves. Barak could not guarantee Deborah's safety, but he understood that if God was with them, and they with him, then they were more likely to experience victory. Their plans would succeed.

Surely, we need to be more concerned with being part of God's victory than building our own reputation or securing our own safety? Whether we are male or female, prioritising our own reputation will distract us from being part of the bigger battles where God makes even bigger purposes. Barak clearly preferred victory in partnership with a woman to defeat with his machismo intact.

It is apparent that Deborah had a mental and spiritual capacity that brought clear battle-strategy, but the author of Judges, who many believe to be Samuel, seems keen to show that women are not without physical strength as well. As mentioned earlier, this battle-story includes Sisera's gruesome death at the hands of a brave, shrewd woman called Jael. This is a powerful story of sweetness and lightning working together to defeat the enemy.

Helen writes:

As young church leaders, one of the first things we did was to appoint leaders with grey hair! This was not so much of a trend preference, rather we looked for some maturity to come alongside our inexperience. We appointed two men. It was not for another three years or so until we learned the wisdom of appointing according to gift before gender, when we appointed an elder who was a woman. She was outstandingly wise and godly and arguably brought the greatest wisdom to strengthen our inexperience as leaders. However, our first team was two male elders who served alongside Tim as the lead elder. The wives were the support team.

After a couple of years of leading the church, these two elders, accompanied by their wives, asked to meet with Tim and myself. We agreed and set up an early morning meeting. After a while, the reason for the meeting became apparent. The four of them wanted to make a point very clear: if Tim was to suddenly die for any reason, they wanted it on record that they would not be looking to me to continue leading the church. Even though we were appointed as *co-leaders* it was important to them that we understand they didn't, and wouldn't, recognise my gift and calling to leadership.

This was a very unusual conversation and one which took us by surprise. Tim's death was not something that we'd particularly considered as a likely possibility. This was not the same for me, though. We had faced the possibility of my death head-on.

Eight weeks after starting to lead the church I had a lumpectomy in my leg. The results were not good. I was diagnosed with secondary terminal cancer and was told that treatment would not be effective and therefore I should prepare to die. Doctors advised us to not have any more children, as leaving Tim with one child would be challenge enough. They also encouraged me to get my affairs in order. This always strikes me as weirdly amusing as I wasn't, and don't intend to have, any affairs! Nonetheless, advice was given and my death was considered a significant possibility.

Our story is seasoned with God's favour, however, and his promise to heal me, spoken four days after my diagnosis, is something he has never reneged on. So while we faced the harsh possibility that Tim might have to parent and lead on his own, our elders wanted assurance that I never would!

Around this table it became apparent that however equal

our call, grace, and anointing (equal, even if not the same), the value placed on them and the opportunities that would come because of them were going more to Tim than myself.

Reflecting on this caused disappointment on many levels, not least for the lack of pastoral concern for me, if I were to be suddenly widowed, but primarily because I allowed this conversation to go unchallenged. We allowed it to remove both of our voices. For the sake of the elders in the room, for honouring them and wanting to be leaders who listened, we did not defend my position, or explore what we might have considered *my* destiny – that is, who I am, rather than who I married.

It would have been impossible to predict if I would have wanted to lead the church in the circumstances of widowhood. But surely that would have been a challenge to journey with the Lord, should that bridge need crossing? I did not stand up for myself, defend myself, or try to argue with our closest team members. I have never wanted to strive for recognition or position and didn't make this a moment to do so. Instead I was silent.

Leadership is not a sexually transmitted anointment, so I didn't become a leader because I got married – otherwise leadership would not be able to be expressed by a single person and that is clearly not the case. I was leading before I was married. However, I have observed that marriage can add a filter to people's perceptions and reinforce a misunderstanding that leadership is essentially and exclusively male. You may get the sense that I have a different view!

At a preaching conference Tim attended, he heard a conversation about male leaders not mentoring women in preaching, for fear of moral failure, or just being misunderstood and tarnishing their witness. For many reasons this is deeply concerning. Such arrogance (assuming that someone would want to have an affair with them), mixed with fear (that their personal weakness might overcome the power of Christ at work in them), linked with unprofessionalism is a concerning cocktail which keeps women restricted and gifts not utilised within the Church and Christian community.

Years later when encouraged to recognise myself as a daughter of Deborah, my heart leapt. Deborah's womanhood, whilst recognised, was not restrictive. She ministered from gift before gender.

Can we become men and women like Barak and Deborah, working together to enable our gifts and strengths, to grow beyond gender stereotypes? Can we go beyond the "control and rule" hierarchy and position-grabbing to discover honest, humble partnership?

Earlier we looked at the garments of grace used to cover Adam and Eve's shame and recognised that they were most likely covering those aspects of their bodies that revealed their sex differences. Their need for each other had been exposed and they tried to cover up the differences between them. The temptation to deny or downplay differences and give into independence and insecurities has been faced by every generation since. However, we should rejoice that our differences make us stronger, together. This story brings that to life.

Before we leave this example of male-female partnership modelled by Deborah and Barak, there a couple of important things to notice.

Firstly, an observation which can't be overlooked. This is the matter of marriage and how it relates to what we're learning. Whilst not much is known about Barak's personal circumstances, there is a simple sentence about Deborah which is highly significant to us as we explore friendly fire. As Deborah is introduced to the reader we learn that, "Deborah, the wife of Lappidoth, was a prophet who was judging Israel at that time."[45] You might think you're not reading anything we've not looked at already, but look again. Another character is introduced to the story. Another relationship is operating within the picture of this restored relationship. Deborah is married to a man named Lappidoth (which means *torch*).

With the introduction of a third character into the story there are some matters we should consider. At no point in the story is there any hint that Deborah's marriage was compromised by her ministry as a prophet, being a mentor to Barak, or accompanying Barak's army into battle. Neither is there a time in the story when Lappidoth steps in and asks for his wife back, or expresses feeling threatened by his wife's working relationship with the leader of the army. Lappidoth is not depicted flexing his muscles, feeling the need to justify his manhood, or defending his role as husband. Perhaps he had more than one wife and was not concerned about the loss of this one? We would choose to give him the benefit of the doubt and rely on the simplicity of the text. Furthermore, at no time in the story is Deborah's integrity questioned, or a suggestion made that a sexual relationship exists between Barak and Deborah. It is not recorded that Barak requests Lappidoth to be present in order to validate their conversations or act as a chaperone. Deborah does not enlist her husband to be present when she works, in order to make sure Barak does not misinterpret her involvement as an opportunity for a sexual encounter, rather than a divine appointment. In fact, throughout this story there do not seem to be any safeguards in place to ensure their relationship is without compromise.

Some might like to argue that Barak is the subject of ridicule for his dependence on a woman. It should not be a point of ridicule that a woman be anointed as a prophet and a leader.

Furthermore, it should not be a point of ridicule when a man makes space for a woman's gift and even depends on it.

Secondly, however scholars may interpret the way the roles in this story are defined and interpreted – and we all read the story through our cultural lenses – isn't it remarkable what we read in Judges chapter 5? What is usually known as the *Song of Deborah* is actually co-authored by Barak.[46] They sang the song of victory, glorifying God for their deliverance, as a duet. We are clearly meant to notice and remember it was teamwork that gave them the victory; a male-female partnership that helped shape their nation's future.

If it is like this in Deborah's, Barak's and Lappidoth's story, could the same be true for our stories? Could we learn something from these heroes of old?

CHAPTER 9
HIM, HER AND THE HARVEST

Helen writes:

If I've been likened to being a daughter of Deborah, not least in my capacity to give a sweet sting (I said it so you don't have to!), then I would consider that I am married to someone who is like a son of my next hero. This story shows us what is possible when men and women humble themselves and serve each other.

The story of Ruth is a fascinating picture of intentionality and generosity. It was possibly written by Samuel, according to Jewish tradition, which explains the prophetic nuances which run through its lines.

The story begins explaining how an Israelite woman, Naomi, came to be living in Moab (home of historical enemies of Israel), widowed and with two widowed daughters-in-law, Orpah and Ruth. Their predicament left them destitute. And so it was that, inspired with hope to return to Naomi's homeland of prospering Judah, the three women set out on a journey. It was not long though, perhaps in response to the arduous journey, that Naomi encouraged her daughters-in-law to leave her and return to Moab. Her motivation was simply to give them a chance of survival and enable them to remarry.

Orpah, through no act of unkindness, took the opportunity and returned home. No more is heard of her. Ruth, however, gave a different response and it is this response that is so fundamental to the story. Ruth the Moabite chooses to become a follower of Naomi's God, Yahweh, when she declares to Naomi, "Wherever you go, I will go, wherever you live, I will live. Your people will be my people, and your God will be my God. Wherever you die, I will die, and there I will be buried. May the Lord punish me severely if I allow anything but death to separate us."[47]

In this pivotal moment Ruth aligns herself with God and with his people. Submitting herself to a higher authority, she turns her back on her history, ancestry and cultural expectations to embark into the unknown journey of faith. Naomi did not return to Bethlehem in Judah as an outcast. She arrived back as a survivor to be warmly greeted and respected. However, while there was no emotional hostility, it would seem that no one came to their immediate aid to provide physical support. In a resilient and industrious fashion, Ruth recognises the opportunity in front of them, having arrived back in the early days of barley harvesting. Ruth sets about meeting their need for food and determines that she will glean discarded grain from the harvesters. This was a custom which, whilst provided for in the law, marked them destitute as a result. There would have been reasons Naomi might have objected to Ruth doing this: for instance, the unwanted attention a foreigner like Ruth might attract, or the shame of having to glean. However, needs must, and the two ladies needed to eat. So Ruth sets out to a field. We, the reader, soon know the owner of the field, but Ruth remains ignorant of this divine providence for a while longer. It's a captivating story.

Ruth refuses to be victim to her circumstances and although willing to die with her mother-in-law, she shows determination to help them both live. She seizes responsibility with both hands as passionately as she seizes the fallen grain from the harvesters, earning the reputation of being a hard worker as well as a woman of integrity.

We must now turn our thoughts to the leading man in this story, Boaz. Boaz is not a young man, as becomes apparent later.[48] He is a wealthy land owner, respected in the community. He comes to inspect his field and the workers one morning and notices Ruth. Boaz's foreman explains who she is and clearly her reputation has spread, as very little introduction is needed: "she is the young woman from Moab who came back with Naomi"[49] seems to be sufficient explanation.

The next turn of events is fundamental to understanding this relationship and its significance. Boaz is duty-bound by Levitical law to allow unharvested crop to be gathered by the poor, foreigners and orphans, with the promise of blessing from the Lord for such a response.[50] So, he invites Ruth to stay within his fields for her own safety, warning his own workers to respect her. He permits her to harvest anything she can whilst walking behind his workers and also says that she can drink the water that his workers draw from the well. He blesses her for her integrity, providing encouragement, comfort (and lunch too!). Boaz however, takes the legal requirement for *obedient generosity* and increases his measure to *voluntary generosity* when he instructs his young farmers to "let her gather grain right among the sheaves without stopping her. And pull out some heads of barley from the bundles and drop them on purpose for her. Let her pick them up, and don't give her a hard time!"[51]

Boaz did not need to give away his harvest to this extent. He chose to generously share what was his. His harvest and his profits were being shared by his choice with this foreign woman. This generosity became a link in this story which in turn enables Boaz to step into his destiny and the next generation to be aligned through him. A profound dynamic is at work here: the generosity of Boaz not only transformed Ruth's experience but positioned him for a providential exchange that would alter his destiny. Boaz was not only being generous to his people, his workers, and his team, he also chose to give away his profits to an unknown woman.

Ruth, blessed, well-fed and protected, works hard each day to gather the grain and returns to Naomi loaded with blessing and with hope rising in her heart. The dialogue between them as they swap stories of the day leads to the tumbling-out of the revelation that, in meeting Boaz, Ruth has stumbled across a close family relative of Naomi's late husband, Elimelech, who is therefore a kinsman and "family redeemer".[52] This means that there is a legal obligation on Boaz towards Naomi.

Ruth, encouraged by Naomi, continues to work in Boaz's field throughout the harvest, but as the harvest season begins to draw to an end, resourceful Naomi begins to consider ways in which she can continue to enable their survival and considers whether there might be a permanent solution for Ruth. The scene that unfolds will show the courage of the women and the integrity of the man.

Instructed by her mother-in-law, Ruth takes a bath, puts on her finest perfume and best clothes and heads to the threshing floor one evening at a time when Boaz will be sleeping, tired from a full day's work and a stomach full of food. Lying by Boaz's feet, which she has uncovered, Ruth rests while Boaz sleeps.[53] Slumber lifts slightly and Boaz stirs to discover, to his surprise, a woman at his feet who was not there when he fell asleep! Asking for someone's identity in that moment is, again, a completely appropriate response. However, when identifying herself, Ruth goes further and actually puts a marriage proposal to Boaz. It might not communicate a request for marriage that anyone would recognise today, but she was a woman of her time and when she says, "spread the corner of your covering over me, for you are my family redeemer"[54] she is employing a local custom for a permanent arrangement! This is not simply a reference to the cold and needing comfort, but an invitation for marriage.[55]

We know that, for some of you, this relationship as an example of a redeemed relationship is losing strength because it is taking a sexual twist. We appreciate the stumbling block. But I urge you to step up and over this for the sake of the journey. Do not let this trip you up, or you will miss the incredible example of Boaz which we can learn from.

Boaz might be excused for responding abruptly out of surprise as he rubbed sleep from his eyes. However, yet again he demonstrates integrity. Choosing not to humiliate or embarrass the woman, instead he reassures her and provides her with enough barley to ensure there is no gossip regarding why she has been in the threshing room overnight. Boaz is committed to not only *doing* the right thing, but being *seen to be doing* the right thing. There is an important lesson to glean from this story: whilst much of this activity occurs behind closed doors, the integrity of what happened in private is maintained in public. Their actions were above repute and gossip could not set in.

The rest of the story unfolds with Boaz going to the only other person who is a possible kinsman, a family redeemer, and honours him with the opportunity of doing the right thing. Whilst this other family member might have wanted to acquire the land and the profits it produced, he was not willing to also take responsibility for the widows. So the opportunity is passed to Boaz. He graciously takes the opportunity and redeems Ruth, marrying her and bringing hope into Naomi's heart and life again.

In a story of ancient practices and symbolic rites of passage, the transaction involves the passing of a symbolic sandal. What is passing hands, though, is not just footwear. A covenant is being made, a partnership formed. Boaz is ensuring that Ruth is not simply discarded like an unwanted item of clothing, but is redeemed like a valuable treasure. He will not allow her to be passed over with the passing away of her former husband, but ensures that she will be provided for and re-established within a family and, as such, in a community. He values her, esteems her, protects and provides for her whilst securing her future. Remember, she is not weak, a broken victim. She is hard working, compassionate, loyal, wise and committed. It was the strength Boaz saw in Ruth that was met by his strength of integrity and willing generosity.

Is this a happy-ever-after ending for the leading characters we've observed? For Ruth and Naomi this might be a perfect conclusion to the story. However, it doesn't end here. God inspires the author to show that he is, again, looking towards a further point in history. This passage ends with this profound paragraph, although we perhaps skip over it too often:

"Perez was the father of Hezron.

Hezron was the father of Ram.

Ram was the father of Ammindidab.

Amminadab was the father of Nahshon.

Nahson was the father of Salmon.

Salmon was the father of Boaz.

Boaz was the father of Obed.

Obed was the father of Jesse.

Jesse was the father of David."[56]

At the end of this story the Lord is allowing dots to be placed on a page which will ultimately stretch for hundreds of years. The dots will be joined to make a glorious picture of salvation and hope as this paragraph is pointing to Jesus himself. To fully grasp this we need to jump to the start of the New Testament, where

Matthew writes Jesus' genealogy, starting with Israel's father of faith, Abraham.[57] When Matthew records this genealogy he recalls "Boaz was the father of Obed (whose mother was Ruth)"[58] concluding his genealogy with the birth of Jesus.[59]

Boaz's response to the Moabite woman's situation resulted in him becoming part of Jesus' genealogy! He not only changed the course of Ruth and Naomi's life, he altered the path of his own destiny and stepped into the genealogy of God's salvation history.

So what can we learn, as leaders, as believers, as members of the church family, from this man and this woman?

Our generosity should go beyond duty and obedience and into audacious choice. Boaz did not just fulfil the law, he surpassed it. Excelling in generosity of protection, provision and propriety, Boaz lavishly gave away his profits.

For us to enter into the fullness of our earthly relationships we should be open handed and generous to not keep things for ourselves. We must fight together against the enemies of injustice and inequality.

At the time of Boaz's generosity, he had no intention of marriage. His focus was not on what he would get, but on what he could give. He was responding to the integrity he saw in the woman and her compassion for God and for his people. He was not only willing for her to pick up the discarded provision, but he was keen for his workers to deliberately create opportunities for her to be provided for and blessed.

Tim writes:

Becoming a Boaz-hearted person means looking at how we can generously *give away*, limiting our own provision, profits and opportunity for the sake of seeing another blessed. As a man, I am deeply convicted by this story, challenged to the core. Generosity doesn't always come easily for us and for sure, one of the challenges of working with others, of building relationships, and especially growing in the context of marriage, is for us men to keep a releasing, generous mindset towards the women in our lives. Whether married or not, I would encourage you to look for opportunities to be generous and dignified in how you treat the women around you; not for what you can get, but for what you can give. If you are married, join with me in the joyous challenge of preferring your wife. Putting her first and encouraging and protecting her dignity with Boaz as a reminder. See from this story how one act of simple generosity and integrity can change the world.

This can and should inform every interaction we have with women in our everyday lives, at work as well as at home.

As for Ruth, she was not motivated by her own survival and her opportunities for future marriage. Instead, she aligned herself with the God of the Israelites. Even though she had suffered a significant loss in bereavement, she was not gripped by despair, nor did she choose to become isolated and self-reliant, establishing herself in such a way that would reduce further heartache by building self-defence around herself. Instead she trusted. We might have understood if she had chosen to create a hard, impenetrable heart that protected her from such searing loss ever being repeated in the future. However, this is not how Ruth copes with her tremendous loss. There is no apparent bitterness taking root. She is a strong-hearted woman without ever being hard-hearted. Ruth could have withdrawn herself from her mother-in-law, but chose instead to align with her, and with her God. In doing so she stepped into line with her destiny and stepped away from yet more division. Amazingly, God's sovereign hand writes her into history, as we saw in Matthew's genealogy. She came, as an unlikely foreigner, and was given a dignified place in the royal line of Jesus' ancestors. What a story!

Ruth showed self-sacrifice, passion, compassion, courage and integrity. She became a servant to reap from what was discarded by others. It was this that positioned her in such a way that her integrity could be observed and her honour and provision came in response.

What a powerful dynamic this is in the battle of the sexes! This generosity crosses the gender divide. Leaders, look around and see who is on the threshing floor of opportunity? Men, instead of just giving opportunities to men, should consider what women are in the threshing field. This could impact all sectors of life.

Ruth did not become a victim of her circumstances or succumb to self-pity. Instead she preferred another identity. She submitted to the will of God and worked hard. Her integrity, compassion, generosity and diligence were matched by Boaz's integrity, compassion, generosity and diligence. Her strong, but not hard, heart, was matched by his strong and generous heart.

When we become more like Boaz and Ruth we will defy the consequences of the curse of Genesis 3:16 and live free from its bondage; no longer subject to the desire to control and rule, but instead, through self-giving love that desires others to succeed, we can resource and release. It is a taste of heaven's unity in this divided world.

This is another victorious partnership that compels us to think again. Can we choose to give away our profit margins? Can we choose to be generous to those around us and maximise their opportunity at the risk of missing out ourselves? Can we allow someone to harvest what we have sown?

CHAPTER 10
HE SPEAKS, SHE RULES, GOD WINS

With the backdrop of Genesis 3:16 in view, we are joining with King David who celebrated in Psalm 16:3 his favourite godly heroes: "The godly people in the land are my true heroes! I take pleasure in them!"

In the battle between the sexes here is another, quite different example, of a victorious partnership: Esther and Mordecai.

This story begins with King Xerxes facilitating the celebrations of his third year of reign for one hundred and eighty-seven days.[61] The last seven days have been a no-limit alcohol-flowing open-invitation party for the Susa Fortress residents. While the king partied with the men, his wife, Queen Vashti, was hosting a palace banquet for the women.[62] Perhaps the king personally abstained from drinking and was totally sobre? As if! It was most likely that, in an over-indulged drunken exhaustion, King Xerxes summoned his wife to come, adorned with her crown, in order to impress his guests with her beauty.[63] The reason why Vashti declines such an invitation is not known. It could be that she simply didn't want to parade wearing her crown, and maybe not much else, in front of a rabble of drunken male guests! Fairly reasonable. Perhaps she was, herself, in no fit state after the festivities to make an appearance? Or maybe she was simply too busy entertaining her own guests. Whatever the reason, her refusal set the king and, in particular his advisors, into a frenzy of fear. The empowerment of the queen to express her opinion and refuse the king's summons could, in their opinion, set a precedent which other wives might follow. The house of cards could fall if women got what they wanted! This in turn could, in their context, encourage men to lose the respect of their wives.

So Queen Vashti is banished and the king "sent letters to all parts of the empire, to each province in its own script and language, proclaiming that every man should be the ruler of his own home and should say whatever he pleases."[64] The war of the ages continues, men and women fighting each other. There is friendly fire all over the place.

King Xerxes is obviously not familiar with the truth of Genesis 3:16, the consequences of that sin-induced curse, or the fact that God does not want husbands to control or rule over their wives. But he can be forgiven. No one who does not love the Lord or respect his laws can be expected to live by them. When the king's anger (and perhaps his hangover) had subsided, regret and loneliness become apparent and in response, the court advisors initiated a plan to "bring beautiful young virgins for the king".[65]

Esther was a young, beautiful Jewish girl who was living in the fortress of Susa with her older cousin, Mordecai. Her parents, who originally named her Hadassah, had died and as a result her cousin Mordecai had adopted her, raising her as his own.[66] Esther, along with many women from across the provinces, is taken to live in the harem accommodation, to be prepared for presentation to the king.

Esther is taken from her family and put in the palace to be primped and preened with a full range of beauty treatments. Nothing is said about the other women who were alongside Esther, but it is apparent that Esther stood out for more than just her beauty with the Harem supervisors.[67] Even though Esther was taken captive against her will, and therefore had much reason to complain and moan, it would appear that she remained soft-hearted and kind towards others in a way that attracted their favour. She received a personally-adjusted menu, her own maids and favourable accommodation. The condition of her heart, much like Ruth, is significant and important to her story and how things pan out for her and all of God's people.

The story of Esther can be deeply concerning, especially considering that she wasn't just entering a beauty pageant – she was entering a one-time-only, full-on audition in the king's bedroom! If we were hearing the story now, in modern times, we would probably conclude that Esther became a victim of human trafficking. Esther was taken, by force, without choice to be prepared for one night of sexual activity with the king. She had all her freedom taken away and was prepared simply for a man's sexual satisfaction. This is surely not dissimilar to the tragic stories we hear of human trafficking nowadays.

It is on this royal stage of tragedy and power-games that God's sovereign hand is seen. A story unfolds which not only reverses the implications of the curse for Esther, but massively impacts the next generation too. The Lord intervenes and brings redemption into the relationships, which ultimately leads to the salvation of a nation, with genocide arrested.

We see great significance in recognising the power and potential of male-female partnerships to bless future generations. This is not in any way limited to baby-making or family-building. It works on so many levels.

Just as the Lord turned this story around for the sake of an entire generation, so we also can see atrocious and tragic human trafficking stories turned around, and a generation rescued for all generations to come when we recognise who the real enemy is and stop the gender war. Women are not possessions to be purchased. Men do not need to validate their manhood or show their worth by oppressing women.

Our dear Ethiopian friend and ministry partner Teklu Wolde was visiting with us recently for a mission's conference. He sat in our lounge with tear-filled eyes as he talked about four women who recently gave their lives to the Lord, but had immediately been "vanished" – i.e. taken without trace. This was, to Teklu, all too familiar. Women are abducted and simply disappear without trace. Someone else treated them like a commodity to be traded, or property to be mistreated or destroyed.

There are many agencies working to rescue such women; women who have been stolen, trafficked and held in atrocious situations against their will. The leader of *Hope for Justice*, Ben Cooley, shared with us once how they celebrate the rescue of every individual woman, each with her own story. They have been part of rescuing infants under the age of one year old, all the way through to a woman in her nineties! You will remember we mentioned the book *Half the Sky*, which has page after page of women's stories filled with tragedy, yet with glimpses of transformation.

Back to Esther: she undergoes twelve months of beauty treatments, submitting to the advisors and doing what she is told. As a result, the beautiful Esther becomes even more beautiful and is favoured by one and all. Every day throughout this year, Cousin Mordecai, still a very significant influence on Esther, visits near the harem to find out what has been happening with her. It does not say that they were able to talk directly, but it is clear he was able to get word to her and his influence on her remained. We read that, "Esther had not told anyone of her nationality and family background, because Mordecai had directed her not to do so."[68]

One year of preparation for one night with the King. It would appear he was so struck by her beauty that he decided to make Esther his queen. Even though now in a royal position, however, Esther "was still following Mordecai's directions, just as she did when she lived in his home."[69]

The sub-plot of the story is that the king's closest advisor, Haman, is jealous of Mordecai, yet ignorant of his familial link with the new Queen Esther. One incident after another leaves Haman wanting Mordecai dead, yet Mordecai is honoured by the king because he foiled a plot to kill the king. So Haman sets out to destroy Mordecai and his people, which of course will entrap the Jewish Queen Esther too.

In his desire to prevent genocide, Mordecai implores Esther to go to the king and reveal the plot against the Jews. Esther protests, telling Mordecai that anyone attempting to visit the king uninvited will be put to death. Moredecai's response is a warning:

"Don't think for a moment that because you're in the palace you will escape when all the other Jews are killed. If you keep quiet at a time like this, deliverance and relief for the Jews will arise from some other place, but you and your relatives will die. Who knows if perhaps you were made queen for just such a time as this?"[70]

This appeal challenges Esther to risk her own life by going uninvited to the king and exposing Haman's unscrupulous scheme.

Because of Esther the Jewish people were saved, Haman was executed, Mordecai was promoted and she remained an influential queen. Yet who would Esther have been without the man Mordecai? Mordecai raised and nurtured her. He then remained in contact with her, advising her, challenging her, observing her as she was raised to the top of the harem and promoted to the most significant role possible: Queen of the land. He remained near her, encouraging her as she battled with this responsibility.

It is notable that when the significance of Esther's position of authority really gripped her heart, she stepped into the opportunity. Esther didn't allow her tender heart to become bitter or hard, even in trying conditions. However, she did allow her heart to grow strong. Growing in resolve, we see that Esther now gives orders to Mordecai for the first time[71] and his response is notable too: "[he] went away and did everything as Esther had ordered him."[72] Mordecai's moment was when he released Esther to be the leader and served in submission to her position. He was side by side with Esther; he recognised her position. Because he saw the God-given placement of his cousin for a purpose, he was willing to follow the Lord's lead and submit to Esther's authority as she took her lead.

The impact of this successful partnership is the next generation being saved. Esther was not simply a pretty puppet. She was a woman who learned to think strategically and recognise opportunity. Esther was able to take advice and give instruction, raise prayer support, and put her own life on the line in order to pursue the greater good. What would have happened if Mordecai hadn't shared the intelligence he'd learned with Esther? What might have happened if Mordecai was too proud to be able to take instruction from Esther to go and gather the community to pray for her? What might have happened if Esther was not willing to realise the opportunity for transformation that was before her?

What a powerful example of synergy, mutual respect, challenge, and of taking turns in leadership under God's sovereign hand! This symbiotic relationship between the man and the woman enabled them to support one another. There was no place for ego or gender-based hierarchy. Instead, there was a recognition of position and purpose. As they were mutually submissive to each other and to the will of God, there was an increase in courage, confidence and an outworking of favour.

This was not ministry in marriage, but through the relationship of mere cousins – a man and woman willing to serve side-by-side with humility. The result? A nation is delivered and God's Kingdom extended. The enemy's scheme against the next generation of God's chosen people was overcome and the course of history was altered in line with heaven's Kingdom plan. Esther was thrust into a situation by human decision, but she recognised the larger divine plan and showed how, in the moment of decision, she rose to the opportunity.

What does this story mean to us? If we want to live in the freedom of the cross and not under the consequences of the curse, then we should humble ourselves and consider the opportunities we face. Rather than clamouring for recognition for ourselves, we must look around – identify others who may be better suited and anointed at this time for influence, not allowing gender to get in the way. Mordecai chose not go to the king directly, because Esther was in fact better positioned to do so. Uniquely positioned. Could there be people near us who are poised for great things that we have not yet prayerfully released into their destiny?

Remember, first, King Xerxes and Queen Vashti. Treating a spouse, or indeed anyone, as a possession is fraught with danger and destined to cause relational failure. Not just in marriage, we might add, but in all areas of human connection. People, are not possessions and trophies to be paraded and boasted about.

Isn't this story remarkable? It starts with the fear of one woman's influence fighting against man, and ends with the celebration of another woman's influence, who works in partnership with a man to overcome evil. Queen Vashti's self-preserving choices led to a season of female oppression. But out of this backdrop rises the story of Esther, leader, queen and a woman who goes on to influence a king and save a generation. Stereotypes and generalisations are fuel for the war between us.

What can we learn and apply from this winning partnership?

There is much to reflect on in terms of the age-old war between men and women. Not a lot has changed. In the corridors and palaces of power all over the world, from mud-huts to mansions, governing bodies and select committees, men and women vie for position. Despite the abuse of political and social power, fuelled by prejudice and the traditions that encourage men and women to fight each other, there is another way.

You don't have to be married, you just need to be willing to recognise the gifting of others; to celebrate their opportunities and successes. Esther and Mordecai show us what it means to fight together and cheer one another on to a victory that is bigger than anyone can take credit for.

The consequences of our victories are further-reaching than we can see. In the end, the famous story of Esther is really about God's careful, sovereign protection of his people from genocide. To him be the glory. Even as we acknowledge this, we thank him that Esther and Mordecai were able to fight together for such a time as this.

In the next section we step into the New Testament, with our eyes wide open, inspired by the examples we've seen and hungry for greater wisdom about how we can live today with dignity, humility and in unity.

Implications and application – some questions

- Which of these stories reveals most to you about what a more full and God-glorifying partnership might look like where you live and serve?
- Can you think of living examples of similar partnerships? What can be learned from them?
- How would you suggest influencers and leaders in your part of the Church respond to this section?

A prayer

Lord of heaven, the only wise God, we humble ourselves before you and thank you for your kindness and daily mercy. Your grace is what we need, as much as ever.

Thank you for the examples of leaders of old who learned to fight darkness together, in partnership, for the blessing of your people and for the sake of your glory.

Help us love and lead like they did and be part of a different kind of community with Christ at the centre.

Holy Spirit, in our day cleanse the Church Jesus died to save – revive us and start with me. Where I have been part of the wrong kind of battle, I ask for your forgiveness and your power to live and bring hope to others. Cleanse me and empower me once again.

And, Lord of peace, may your people together show those around us what you are like.

In Jesus' name.

Amen.

Section 4: Empire and Kingdom – a new way to rule

As we step into the New Testament we can see all around the ancient world the damage caused by centuries of empire-building. Palaces and places of worship destroyed, refugees in exile, generations of heartache. Men in their pride and independence, with their lust for riches and power, are joined by women and their desire to self-govern. This lethal combination has caused havoc over the ages. It's a blood-soaked scene and, as we survey it, we can identify so much with our own world. We seem hell-bent on rejecting God's rule and literally leading our own lives. We want to be the arbiters of our own destiny and overpower others along the way.

The prophets spoke to the powers of their day and began to sing the song of a new kingdom to come. They pronounced that a time would come when dignity would return to humanity, because humanity would return to God. Isaiah, Amos, Ezekiel and Jeremiah were amongst those who foretold of a Davidic king who would restore heaven's authority on the earth. Whilst they imagined in most cases the reestablishment of the Temple in Jerusalem and the coming of a military ruler, Isaiah caught a glimpse of the Messiah, the Suffering Servant, who would come in humility, initiating an eternal kingdom the likes of which had not yet been seen:

"For a child is born to us,

a son is given to us.

The government will rest on his shoulders.

And he will be called:

Wonderful Counsellor, Mighty God,

Everlasting Father, Prince of Peace.

His government and its peace will never end.

He will rule with fairness and justice from the throne of his ancestor David for all eternity.

The passionate commitment of the Lord of Heaven's Armies will make this happen!"[73]

An eternal kingdom of peace is coming, of fairness and justice, and the child born will lead the way for sure.

Here comes Jesus.

All earthly empires will come and go, but the kingdom he ushers in will be of a different quality altogether. Here is where we see the potential for the wars between us to end. Not least the battle of the sexes.

John writes in chapter 3 of his gospel, v16-21:

"For this is how God loved the world: He gave his one and only Son, so that everyone who believes in him will not perish but have eternal life. God sent his Son into the world not to judge the world, but to save the world through him. There is no judgment against anyone who believes in him. But anyone who does not believe in him has already been judged for not believing in God's one and only Son. And the judgment is based on this fact: God's light came into the world, but people loved the darkness more than the light, for their actions were evil. All who do evil hate the light and refuse to go near it for fear their sins will be exposed. But those who do what is right come to the light so others can see that they are doing what God wants."

After centuries of darkened and often-deadly battle between men and women vying for position and power in the kingdoms of the earth, the promised Messiah is here; shining light on our brokenness, restoring the human community. He ushers in the Kingdom of God. Self-rule makes way for God's rule and the way in for this is self-sacrifice. Profoundly, the means by which Jesus inaugurates the new kingdom is self-emptying love; self-giving service. As Paul famously demonstrates in Philippians 2:5-11,

"You must have the same attitude that Christ Jesus had.
Though he was God,
he did not think of equality with God
as something to cling to.
Instead, he gave up his divine privileges;
he took the humble position of a slave
and was born as a human being.
When he appeared in human form,
he humbled himself in obedience to God
and died a criminal's death on a cross.
Therefore, God elevated him to the place of highest honour
and gave him the name above all other names,

that at the name of Jesus every knee should bow,
in heaven and on earth and under the earth,
and every tongue declare that Jesus Christ is Lord,
to the glory of God the Father."[74]

Paul prescribes a new attitude: the posture of Christ who put others first, humbled himself, and empowers us to do the same. What Jesus accomplished in all this was to establish a kingdom that supersedes all human empires, now and forever.

Building on what we have been exploring so far in this book, this section will call us into the new heavenly light of God's kingdom-on-earth, made possible because of the incarnation of Jesus into our broken world. What happens to the gender war when the Kingdom of God is at hand? Here is Jesus, born as a male into a patriarchal Jewish society, showing us a new way of dignity and humility, strength and social courage.

CHAPTER 11
WOMEN ON THE WAY (NOT IN THE WAY)

Tim writes:

It was a pretty awkward moment to be fair. It usually is when someone points out the blatantly obvious in a moment of vulnerability. Ron Corzine, a dear friend and confidante, an apostolic consultant and spiritual father, has been one of the men in our lives that God has used the most strategically to nudge us forward. We had not long moved into The Wellspring Church Centre and some painful, yet important changes had been made to help us move forward as a church family. We had expanded to two Sunday services, the congregations were growing, but my half-developed management skills were really not helping us keep up with the changes taking place. In some areas of church life my wisdom had run out.

So there we were, with Ron, sitting in our lounge after a leaders meeting, talking about what God wanted to do and identifying what needed to happen for our vision to be fulfilled. Helen was her usual bright, cheerful and lucid self, and I was applying all the wisdom I could to find a way forward. Two or three times Helen identified and said things that sounded obvious when she said them, because they were so full of wisdom, and they wiped the floor with the best I could bring. After a few of these wise pearls, Ron looked at me and said something like, "Listen to this: she is so much wiser than you, Tim! Your church needs more of this – the best of her time and abilities, focused on your mission together." Ron encouraged us to get over the obstacles that were preventing Helen joining our staff team. He urged us to climb through the hedge of presumptions and misunderstanding that were in danger of holding our whole church back.

A similar moment took place a year or two later. Robin Sanderson, a dear friend and insightful member of our leadership team, had probably been Helen's biggest fan on our team. He encouraged and championed her ever-improving study and preaching. He was able to discern the differences between Tim and Helen's shared leadership and Mr and Mrs Roberts' loving marriage. At the end of a Senior Leadership Team meeting he got me to stand up so I could be prayed for. He stated that until this time it was my leadership that had been to the fore, and that God had used me to bring us this far. Then he placed his hand on Helen's shoulder and stepped her forward, by my side. Robin then declared, with simple yet prophetic clarity, that now we were to lead together, and this would unlock blessing and growth in the church. He re-enacted this later, in a public meeting, and it was received by church members with prayerful applause. We have sought to live in response to this word ever since. We thank God for the wisdom of men like Ron and Robin, to encourage us to see our partnership as heaven intended it.

What had been holding us back from recognising Helen's gifts and abilities? Was part of it a misunderstanding, even selective memory, about how Jesus treated women? It's to that we'll turn next…

Jesus described himself as the way, the truth and the life.[75] Without him we are simply unable to come to the Heavenly Father. So at the centre of our Christian faith, is Jesus. He is the Son of God and yet also Son of Man. He is the true "vine"[76] in which we must remain to be fruitful and to have life, and so we could continue. Most likely we don't need to convince you that Jesus must be central to our understanding of how God wants us to form and invest in human relationships, not least how we relate as men and women. It must be through the lens of his life, teaching and sacrifice that we read the Old Testament and interpret the world around us today. Therefore, what Jesus said *about* women and *to* women, along with how he personally *related* to women should form and challenge how we are to relate one to another today. That's what we'll explore here.

Church leadership is far from easy. Our experience is that the joys and challenges of leading God's people take you to extreme places emotionally, mentally and spiritually. Most leaders start out intending to do the right thing and make godly decisions in every interaction with those they lead and associate with. As leaders we want to get things right and show God's love to people every time. We look at the example of Jesus and how he led his disciples and the wider group who followed him, and we are amazed and in awe of his grace. We admire his wisdom and want to follow his lead in addressing racial and social division. Here is our Saviour, who partied with the marginalised and criticised the bigoted.

So what do we learn of Jesus' approach to the women in his world?

Stepping into biblical equality in our relationships between male and female can surely not be done without an appreciation for what Jesus said and did. Like us, you might have heard the argument (mostly made by male leaders) that because Jesus only chose twelve male disciples, then leaders of apostolic authority or standing should only be male. Some then deduce that every church leadership team today should be exclusively male. They need to think again.

Back then Jesus only chose *Jewish* leaders, so should that limit who we can have on our leadership teams just as much? Plus, the Twelve were most likely all under eighteen years old too. Does that mean today all of our church leadership teams should consist exclusively of male, Jewish teenagers? Of course not! We would suggest that there are social, symbolic and practical (rather than doctrinally prescriptive) reasons why Jesus the Rabbi selected these young men as his closest followers.

With a wider lens attached to the life and work of Jesus – where we step back and see how he lived and walked on this earth – we see him challenging men's subjugation of women. He came to show mankind "The Way" which he himself personified and which marked out a path for us to follow. One question that occurs to us is: *was Jesus, the sinless man, able in this darkened, battle-torn world to build relationships that were free of the consequences of the curse?* As the light that breaks into the darkness of the wars between us, we see that even before he had won the ultimate victory on the cross and through the empty tomb, Jesus demonstrated how men and women can, should and will relate in his kingdom.

Even before Jesus was born, we see a sign. Even while in the womb, the Holy Spirit was highlighting the significance of the Christ-child. His presence was confirmed by the pre-natal movement of his cousin, John, carried by his aunt Elizabeth. Luke's Gospel uses Elizabeth being filled with the Holy Spirit to confirm that Mary and her unborn child were blessed of God.[77] It is worth noting that Jesus' significance could have been confirmed through a man, yet it was confirmed through the prophetic movement of a baby boy within a woman's womb. Let's think about that for a moment and wonder. Given that God in his infinite power and ineffable wisdom could have chosen a different means of entering this earth and achieving salvation for humankind, isn't it a marvel that he chose a woman's womb to care-take the Messiah for nine months? In the gospel story, the first human God trusted is a woman. The first person to bring a prophetic confirmation that Mary was carrying the Christ was Elizabeth, a woman. The most precious life ever to enter our world, when at his most vulnerable, was entrusted to the natal care of a young girl. Her womb and her gender gloriously dignified by the divine.

Soon after Jesus' birth he was presented, in accordance with the Jewish custom, at the Temple. It was there that Luke's Gospel recalls the prophetic confirmation of this newborn's significance through the prophecy of Simeon, and then in a simple but profound way through the confirming praise of Anna.[78] Anna was an elderly widow who devoted herself to a life of prayer and was recognised for her gift of prophecy. She spent many hours in the Temple. It is not clear whether she was in residence within a charitable alms house or as a consulting prophetess, or was just living locally and regularly attending the Temple to pray. Either way, she was a devoted, respected and gifted woman who overheard Simeon's declaration that this babe-in-arms was indeed the awaited Messiah. The one to spread the word, confirm the prophecy and gossip this good news was Anna, a woman, given a voice by God in a Temple dominated by men. We'll pick this up later – how profound it is that the most important news ever told is not simply for men to share. Notably, in announcing and ushering in the Kingdom of God, his chosen mouthpiece is as likely to be a woman as a man.

Many a modern family would be able to imagine the scene of a son being encouraged to do something they don't want to do by their mother. "Oh Mu-um!" exclaimed with the shrug of the shoulders or the bang of a door. Most sons recognise that at times it is really hard to give in and do what your mum asks you to do. In fairness, daughters don't always do well on this either!

In John's Gospel we see the first miracle of Jesus in public and he is being encouraged to do it by his mother! Not keen, he tries to shrug it off, but she presses the point. Jesus and his mother are at a wedding when the supply of wine is running dry. Mary senses the stress of the servants, and possibly the hosts, and instructs the servants to speak with Jesus. He emphatically tells her that it is not his concern and that he is not ready to begin any public ministry. Mary does not relent. Instead, she simply tells people to do what he says.

Jesus could have ignored, dismissed or quietened Mary. Instead he submits to her insistence and does what she asks. We love the fact that Mary knew Jesus could have done something about it. How many times in his childhood had Mary seen her son do extraordinary things? How many glimpses did she have of his supernatural power? Back to the wedding. Out of confidence in who her son was and what he could do, Mary nudges Jesus into his public ministry, apparently ahead of its due time. The Saviour of the World is subject to, in submission to, his mother, a woman.

There is an incredible story in the fourth Gospel where a nameless woman encounters Jesus at a well. This is a beautiful and profound episode which Kenneth E. Bailey brings to life brilliantly in his book *Jesus Through Middle Eastern Eyes*. The custom of the day was that men would not talk to women in public unless they were their wife or family, and even then scarcely. Dialogue with women would have been reserved to private accommodation. Yet Jesus was not going to be limited to this gender-challenge and instead impacted this one woman's world and arguably all women following. Cultural expectations meant that Jesus should have moved out of the way of the well when the woman approached. However he did not budge. He stayed in her way.

The well and the bucket are incredibly significant as Bailey explains: "Middle Eastern wells do not have buckets attached to them. Each traveling group must have its own... Crossed sticks in the top keep the soft leather mouth open to allow the bucket to fill as it is lowered into the well. When not in use the traveller can roll up the bucket for transport. The text assumes that Jesus and the disciples had such a bucket, but the disciples had taken it with them to the city. Jesus could easily have requested that they leave it behind for his use. But he had a plan."[79]

Jesus needed his disciples, and their resources, out of the way in order to show how he needed the resources of a woman instead. Does this not make your heart race at the thought that, as a disciple of Christ, there might be times when he simply needs us out of the way in order that he can do the miracles to further his Kingdom and let his will be done? Just to emphasise the point, when the disciples returned with the food they were sent for, their mission was undermined as largely irrelevant as Jesus' hunger had been satisfied through his work with "a kind of food you know nothing about."[80] He no longer needed what his disciples had. Their mission for food was simply to get them out of the way. Are any of us in the way of what God wants to do?

Whilst Jesus was asking for something from the woman, he then gave her something even greater: he revealed truth, love and destiny. When she left his presence she was inspired, arguably as an evangelist and preacher, to bring transformation and revival. Of course, Jesus could have gone himself to the village and started preaching. He could have gone with his disciples and begun healing, delivering and teaching, which would have led to the salvation of many. Instead, he wanted to elevate a woman, providing a landmark moment that sent a woman as a breakthrough "apostle" to transform a village. This is a message that should make a difference to us now. Of course she wasn't given a badge or a label or a department; she was given something much more profound: she was given *permission*. She was sent. Tradition has it that this woman, St Photina, continued fearlessly to preach the gospel in Samaria and beyond, along with her sons. She ended up martyred by the evil Emperor Nero who threw her skinless down a well. From the initial encounter with Christ, it is understood the Samaritan woman lived a dedicated life to reaching hundreds, even thousands, with the good news.

Think about what this tells us. If Jesus could receive from a woman and also send her out as catalyst for transformation, cannot the other male followers of Christ do the same?

Have you ever watched TV adverts and considered who their target market is? There are times when the specific subtleties of adverts are wasted on us because we're not their target market. We are not inspired by what they are trying to sell, promote and tell us is a must-have item. The best marketers have worked out not only what they are promoting, but who they want to promote it to. This in turn influences every choice that is made when creating the advert – the language and style and means of communication. The same is true in any public speaking situation. Knowing your audience and speaking in a way that communicates to them is essential if the message is going to get across.

Jesus is surely the best communicator of all time and he recognised that he needed to adapt what he was saying to his target audience. Jesus wanted to communicate with women as much as he wanted to communicate with men. Furthermore, Jesus intentionally adapted his teachings in order to communicate his message as powerfully to women as to men; often bringing parables and teachings around the story of both a woman and a man. The widow at Zarapeth, for instance, is taught in the same breath as the healing of Naaman.[81] Bailey observes how Jesus brought parables with illustrations that would resonate with an audience of men and women with the "twin parables of the mending of the garment (the task of a woman) and the making of wine (the work of men)."[82] Similarly the parable of the mustard seed would capture the understanding of the male audience, as men were typically the farmers, but it is linked directly to the story of the woman kneading the dough.[83] Jesus was profoundly and intentionally inviting men *and* women into his heavenly kingdom.

In Luke's Gospel we hear of Jesus visiting his friends, Mary, Martha and Lazarus. He was to receive the hospitality of Martha, who was preparing the guests a "big dinner",[84] however the host begins to resent that she is the only one rushing around doing the work. Her sister Mary was "sat at the Lord's feet, listening to what he taught".[85] In those days, to sit at the feet of someone was to show that you were their disciple and they were your Rabbi, teacher. Mary was opting out of her traditional responsibilities and duties and instead doing what men would typically do: sitting, listening and entering into the dialogue with Jesus. When Martha complains about the division of the traditional labour, Jesus is heard "defending Mary's right to become his disciple and continue her 'theological studies'. The traditional cultural separation between men and women no longer applies."[86]

Furthermore, Jesus is showing that even in the context of a domestic-private setting, he was willing to teach women – even though it could risk scandal, to do so in a private rather than a public context. As a rabbi, Jesus was willing to teach women. Just as he wanted his male students to not only be hearers but do-ers of the word, so too was his expectation for his female students. Jesus was turning the patriarchal system on its head and bringing it back in line with his heavenly Father's created order. Mary was opting to use her brain and her heart rather than her domestic capabilities on this occasion. And Jesus not only allowed it, he affirmed it, saying to Martha, "My dear Martha, you are worried and upset over all these details! There is only one thing worth being concerned about. Mary has discovered it, and it will not be taken away from her."[87] Jesus affirmed a woman's right to be a disciple and not to be relegated solely to domestic affairs.

This is our overarching point, our affirmation: Jesus associated with women, talked with women, socialised with women, allowed women to support him financially, to pour expensive ointment on him, prophesised over women, shared a cup with women, healed women, honoured women and made sure his mother was cared for after his death, even while hanging on a cross. He revealed his resurrected body first to women and generally lived his life to demonstrate with words and deeds that salvation through him was for women as well as men. In a patriarchal society, a "kingdom of this world", Jesus inaugurated a new kingdom with a new set of values and, not least, established a more heavenly way of dealing with women and encouraging mutual respect and synergy between the sexes. Women are not in the way of Jesus' kingdom mission. They are essential and necessary partners on The Way as heaven's values are expressed amongst God's people on the earth.

CHAPTER 12
DON'T FORGET THE MESSENGER

We've been looking at the convention-breaking Way of Jesus in this gender war. As we gather our thoughts, it is worth noting a few things: The twelve apostles were all men and there is no evidence to suggest that any of the seventy disciples who were sent out were women. This is not surprising, given the social conditions of the times he was living in. However, women *were* Jesus' disciples, receiving teaching, being part of his mission and also financiers of the mission from their own resources. Once Jesus' ministry was underway – known by the early Church as The Way – and many more people were joining, it is fascinating how Luke describes his support base at the start of Luke 8:

"Soon afterward Jesus began a tour of the nearby towns and villages, preaching and announcing the Good News about the Kingdom of God. He took his twelve disciples with him, along with some women who had been cured of evil spirits and diseases. Among them were Mary Magdalene, from whom he had cast out seven demons; Joanna, the wife of Chuza, Herod's business manager; Susanna; and many others who were contributing from their own resources to support Jesus and his disciples."[88]

Isn't it fascinating how intrinsically connected both men and women are to Jesus' ministry? His entourage is mixed gender. Not only that, women business leaders provided essential resources to support this travelling ministry as it gained momentum and influence. They had clearly left their homes and were part of the travelling party, following Jesus. This might not be staggering to us now in a contemporary setting, but in the traditional setting of Jesus' day, women were allowed to travel with men during the day but would need to stay with relatives at night. Whilst he could have depended on the financial support of Galilean fishermen alone, Luke explains that Jesus and his team depended on the resourcefulness and generosity of influential women. Our Lord and Saviour gathered and used leaders and resources without preference of gender. There is a lesson here, made even more profound by the fact that Luke, a man, includes this detail when recounting the story.[89]

Look forward to the cross and here we are again. Jesus is in his most vulnerable place and it is faithful women who are at his feet. It was the women who stayed with Jesus right up until his last breath, when most of the men had fled in fear. There is such dignity and grace on display here. See the strength of these women as they watch their Lord give up his life. According to Matthew, Jesus' mother, Mary the mother of James and Joseph, and also the mother of the sons of Zebedee are there.[90] Mark echoes this, emphasising the faithful presence of women at the cross[91] – something we should not overlook.

Whilst some might suggest the women only held a peripheral role at the burial scene, it is clear that they played a more significant part in the resurrection scene, as other than the women it is only an angel who is initially present at the empty tomb. Please join us in wonder at this quite simple and obvious fact: *Jesus chose to reveal himself, in resurrected form, first to a woman.*

At a time in history when the testimony of a woman was not considered valid, Jesus enabled a woman's testimony to corroborate his resurrection first.

Jesus chose to reveal his resurrected body first to women and to have his angels commission them to "go quickly and tell his disciples that he has risen from the dead, and he is going ahead of you to Galilee. You will see him there. Remember what I have told you."[92] The. Most. Important. Message. Ever. Told. Entrusted to a woman.

Mary is commissioned to both declare Jesus' resurrection and also pass on some crucial instructions to the apostles. Don't ignore the messenger! In this sense, could Mary be understood as an apostle to the apostles – at least for this moment? Either way, if an apostle of Christ is someone who carries the message of Christ to the world, then surely Mary at Jesus' resurrection, and earlier the Samaritan woman at the well, both carried the good news of Christ as "sent ones". It is worthy of our consideration. There is no hint of a divine instruction to "wait for a man" to share this truth with authority – the greatest news ever shared by any human on the planet: "He is risen!"

Some of today's church structures and approaches to recognising and appointing leaders have sadly fallen away from the Garden Tomb principle. As if some would say, "This message/ role/responsibility is way too important for just anyone. We need a man to carry this burden!" Instead, the risen Jesus walking in the garden is delighted to see a person he trusts, a woman, and he sends her out in this pivotal moment to offer leadership to us all.

Bailey puts this so brilliantly when he says, "this movement on the part of the women, out of the shadows of the accounts of the cross and burial and into the bright light of Easter morning, is a fitting climax to the dramatic affirmation of the radical equality of men and women, the fellowship that Jesus created."[93]

Biblical equality is often limited within the Church because leaders are unsure whether all roles and responsibilities can be handed to women with biblical integrity. Debates and votes have been argued and cast. As we said before, there are some interesting things to note about the twelve apostles. For those who contend that disciples, apostles, evangelists, preachers, teachers, etc., can only be men (because Jesus chose only men to be his apostles), they must also conclude that they must all be Jewish, because he only chose Jewish men. Yet we apply our understanding of the whole Scripture that breaks down the religious barrier to extend to Gentiles. Or as Williams comments, we do not hear people say that, "because Jesus did not appoint any black men as disciples, they can't be apostles either!"[94] We should not be free in part, but wholly free to embrace the truth expressed in Paul's letter to the Galatians:

"...all who have been united with Christ in baptism have put on Christ, like putting on new clothes. There is no longer Jew or Gentile, slave or free, male and female. For you are all one in Christ Jesus. And now that you belong to Christ, you are the true children of Abraham. You are his heirs, and God's promise to Abraham belongs to you."[95]

So what have we discovered about women on The Way? We must remember that Jesus modelled an intentional discipleship of both genders – a mentoring of women alongside his mentoring of men.

Implications and application – some questions

- In what way does this exploration of Jesus' approach to women challenge your own feelings of superiority/inferiority in this gender war?

- Think about your own experiences in the church. How do you deal with the damaging actions of others or even your own sense of responsibility for how you have treated others?
- What would the impact be on our wider communities today if men in the Church treated women more like Jesus did in the first century?

A prayer

Loving Father, lover of our souls, thank you for Jesus. Thank you for sending him to mend the rift between us and you, and between us and each other. By your Spirit, make us more like him. May we reflect the love, grace and mercy of Christ in all our actions and reactions, today and always.

For your name's sake,

Amen.

Section 5: Paul: Marmite-Man

One advertising campaign that we might well be the target market for is for that weirdly-wonderful product called *Marmite*! A sticky, dark brown food paste made from yeast extract, it has a distinctive, powerful flavour, which is extremely salty and, apparently, deeply divisive. Its marketing campaign capitalised on the fact that people either "love it or hate it". It would seem that only one of those responses is appropriate.

Paul is a bit of a Marmite-man. When it comes to understanding biblical equality in the context of the twenty-first century, Paul can come across badly and end up loathed. However, we cannot avoid the challenge of grappling with what he did say, to understand how we really should live. Paul holds the position of being (with the exception, of course, of Jesus) the most influential New Testament leader and the most prolific writer, exceeding all of Jesus' initial disciples including Peter, the Rock whose faith-confession was foundational for the Church.

What Paul says is important. So whether this Marmite-man fills you with hope or horror, it's time to spread his words (did you see what we did there?)

Of all the sections in this book, this is the heaviest. We appreciate that it will look like we're attempting to be more academic than we have in other sections and we urge you to not let this put you off. Stick with this journey. It will be worth it! We simply cannot have a woolly faith. It is Paul's teaching in particular that can provide the greatest stumbling block to us understanding biblical equality, but it shouldn't. These verses should be a stepping-stone to a greater understanding and Holy Spirit-inspired freedom. In tackling some of these verses we will reveal the enemy's strategy, that has resulted in us causing one another wounds by so called friendly-fire, rather than by tackling and defeating our real enemy, through Christ.

So please stick with us. We can get through this together!

CHAPTER 13
LETTERS OF LOVE OR THE POISONED PEN?

Our bookstores, both digital and physical, are filled with examples of how freed people become freedom-fighters. Obese people lose weight and become authors and dieticians to help others; convicted criminals spend time in jail and then use their freedom helping others avoid their pitfalls; parents in crisis struggle through, gaining wisdom they can share with others, helping them succeed where others have failed; former addicts help to encourage and support others; business achievers show the journey from rags to riches, from market minnows to corporate dragons. Self-help books abound to help us improve our lives! The Bible is similar in that the journey of the authors or their subjects have gone from victim to victor, oppressor to liberator. Consider Moses, Joseph and David and, of course, many of the people referred to in this book. We can see that lives can be turned around, so that trials become testimonies.

So it is with the Apostle Paul. In the book of Acts and through his letters we see him addressing principles and truths of the freedom that comes as a true follower of Christ. However, he journeyed from his devoutly religious roots, as an oppressor and suppressor of the early followers of Christ, into a revelation encounter with God that left him transformed and passionate about a relationship with Jesus. He became a liberator! Paul is totally committed to a message of freedom. Furthermore, in his writing and preaching he strives to uphold the value of unity; unity amongst believers and unity in the Spirit.

Paradoxically, his words have been understood by some to encourage significant division, especially between the sexes. It is his words that are often quoted when trying to understand the roles and relationship between women and men, which seem to force a divisive wedge between them. Furthermore, his teaching is too often used as a proof text by those who inadvertently (and sometimes knowingly) further the suppression of others, in particular women. We're obviously not in a position to ask Paul about this personally, but we would deduce that to have his words used to suppress, divide and subjugate in this way, would sadden and exasperate him.

To bring an end to the damage caused through gender-related friendly-fire and find true biblical synergy, we must not avoid the controversy surrounding Paul's writings. As we consider the relationships between male and female, and discover whether we are living in the shadow of the curse or the light of the cross, we need to embrace Paul's teaching and understand his context: what he was writing *then* and what it might mean for us *now*. The battle of the sexes sadly rages on in both obvious and hidden places – from public platforms in church to private prejudices and "discrete" conversations. Will we hear Paul's trumpet call? His appeal for true synergy amongst God's people?

If we consider other streams of Paul's teaching – such as regarding slavery, for example – we can see a progressive liberty and freedom in our understanding, over time. There is a trajectory of teaching which enables us to understand our application today. Grace and caution must be applied, of course, to not add some dots on the paper – like a badly formed dot-to-dot puzzle that is missing some links – so that we don't conclude something was never meant to be there. We must read each text within the context of the time and season that it was written. But with Paul's teaching on slaves in mind, very few of us think that we must acquire ourselves a slave, so that we can help them live for Christ as a slave and fulfil Paul's teaching! Nor do we support those who do keep slaves and preach to the slave that they should remain in that circumstance. Rather, when the slave trade (which is still tragically very much alive) is mentioned, we rightly respond with outrage and demand that action be taken to halt its increase.

Sadly, Paul's teaching on women is not always treated with the same maturity. We don't always apply the same wisdom and historical context to understanding what he is saying. We don't consider his whole teaching and lifestyle in order to grasp the full message.

When it comes to Paul's teaching on men and women, we must tread with care, uphold the truth and not become confused. Mines have been laid on this battleground and friendly-fire war wounds abound. This teaching has become divisive between the genders in some places. The resulting legacy means that the consequences of the curse and judgement are operating across generations, hindering the release of women into ministry by restricting the function of their gifts and calling. This is holding men back too from enjoying and embracing the fruits of co-equal synergy. Just as the enemy put doubt into Eve and misled her in the Garden of Eden, questioning "Did God really say?"[96] so we should go back to the truth, rejecting confusion, and establish what God *really did say* through Paul about how men and women should live and serve in the Church.

The way in which men and women relate to one another is directly impacted by our understanding of how God chooses to gift us. Exploring whether women can lead, teach and preach, for example, is intrinsically important to stepping into biblical equality. In this section we're going to tackle some hot-potatoes! A few verses in some of Paul's letters have been used with the effect that women's function within church, home and society have been restricted. In particular, Paul's letters to the church in Corinth and also to the leader of the church in Ephesus, Timothy.

Let us invite you into our home for a minute. Imagine this hypothetical scene... it's a Saturday morning. This is our one occasional opportunity for a lie-in. A rare chance to stay in bed and allow our bodies the chance to sleep until they're done! Whilst we have children and they operate as alarm clocks in their own right, we know that we cannot respond by bumping them on the head like a snooze button! So imagine first, one of our daughters bounds into the room at 6.00am: "Can I get up now?'" In a soporific state we reply, "No, our lovely daughter, you may not get up before 7.30am this morning, as it is right for you to honour your parents with silence in the house." She returns to her room and goes back to bed. Soon after, at 6.15am, our son leaps from his bed with a thud (he used to have a raised bed... so the landing was always loud). "Wake up and listen to my drumming. I have a new beat I've been practising." We reply, "No son, it is not right for you to play your drums for us. We are not going to listen to your new beats. Instead you must be silent!"

These are surprisingly articulate responses, given that we were just sleeping. They are also highly unlikely in order to make a point. Did our response mean that our daughter may never be permitted to get up before 7.30am, *ever*? Of course not, or she would be repeatedly late for school or (gasp in horror) church! If this was written down and read by another family, would they understand that it is good practice that no daughter in any household be allowed to rise before 7.30am? Did we mean that our son is *always* to be silent and that we would *never* listen to him play his drums? If this instruction was read by another family, would they understand that no boy should ever play drums?

Of course not, that would be ludicrous. Plus, if you knew our son you would know that would be practically impossible! It is simply something we said on one occasion that was related to a specific context. To fully understand what was meant, others would need to know the context of our situation – the time of day, the busyness of our schedule, our need for rest, our children's need to be trained to let us rest! As well as this immediate context, we could add that such a response will be for a season only, after which it will be irrelevant – especially considering the rapid advance of our children's years and their teenage ability to sleep way beyond any lie-in that we might enjoy.

Conrad Gempf writes in his book *How to Like Paul Again* that we need to understand that Paul is writing letters to people in particular contexts. We are effectively reading someone else's mail. Paul's letters were not "written for everyone, but for the specific people they were addressed to."[97] He continues to liken it to listening to one side of a telephone conversation which, when we realise this, helps us to understand we are trying to fill in the gaps of a conversation we have not been privy to.

It would be wrong to base an entire theory on just two statements, taken out of context, referring to only one half of a conversation. So too, we must not build a whole theology and ecclesiology without understanding the context in which Paul's words were written. Let's now look at these controversial passages of Scripture and try to understand what they are really saying to us, both men and women.

Chapter 14
Heads or tails – Corinth

Paul's first letter to the Corinthians was written some time after he had first visited them, around the mid-point of the first century. Corinth was an ancient Greek city, connecting the mainland section of Greece with the provinces of Macedonia and Epirus. The city had been demolished by the Romans and later rebuilt at the instruction of Julius Caesar in 44BC. Many slaves were freed as a result of the rebuilding in return for military service and, as a result, the population was very loyal to Rome. The city prospered and the Isthmian Games, a significant sporting and cultural festival, took place there every two years. Trade, travel and tourism led to the cosmopolitan development of the city. Politics flourished in this environment and the two ports serving the city employed a large population of manual workers. Former slaves enjoyed freedom and opportunity and some rose to high public office. Cults also thrived there, creating a religiously diverse community. It was into this environment that Paul arrived to minister the gospel.

Let's dive into one of the key passages:

3 "But there is one thing I want you to know: The head of every man is Christ, the head of woman is man, and the head of Christ is God. 4 A man dishonours his head if he covers his head while praying or prophesying. 5 But a woman dishonours

her head if she prays or prophesies without a covering on her head, for this is the same as shaving her head. 6 Yes, if she refuses to wear a head covering, she should cut off all her hair! But since it is shameful for a woman to have her hair cut or her head shaved, she should wear a covering.

7 A man should not wear anything on his head when worshiping, for man is made in God's image and reflects God's glory. And woman reflects man's glory. 8 For the first man didn't come from woman, but the first woman came from man. 9 And man was not made for woman, but woman was made for man. 10 For this reason, and because the angels are watching, a woman should wear a covering on her head to show she is under authority.

11 But among the Lord's people, women are not independent of men, and men are not independent of women. 12 For although the first woman came from man, every other man was born from a woman, and everything comes from God.

13 Judge for yourselves. Is it right for a woman to pray to God in public without covering her head? 14 Isn't it obvious that it's disgraceful for a man to have long hair? 15 And isn't long hair a woman's pride and joy? For it has been given to her as a covering. 16 But if anyone wants to argue about this, I simply say that we have no other custom than this, and neither do God's other churches.[98]

First, let us consider the meaning behind Paul's use of the expression *head*, where he said Christ is the head of a man, but not the head of a woman. Instead, the head of a woman is a man. Of course, Paul was writing in Greek, so we have to look deeper for understanding and correct translation. The Greek word used for what we read as *head* was *kephale*. As Hewitt succinctly summarises in his book *The Gender Revolution*, our understanding of this word is crucial in its context and open to misinterpretation. We are in good company with respected scholars who deduce that Paul here is not primarily describing a hierarchy or authority. Some read into this passage a subordination of women under men and "head" is taken to mean "master" or "lord". We assert that here Paul is not affirming man's authority over woman, but perhaps a better translation of "head" is source.

The sequence described in verse 3 may not be hierarchical, but rather chronological.[99] Whenever he gets the opportunity, Paul seems to want to take readers back to God's original plan, expressed in Genesis. Paul is concerned about the drift that happens amongst believers, when we forget the intention of the Creator. So perhaps he is simply outlining a reminder of the creation story? This helps us a little, but it is not fully satisfactory as an explanation, when considering the statement that the head of Christ is God. What could this mean?

Let's think about this further. One thing to consider is the actual physical head of a person. Very few of us are able to recognise people by their body alone. For this context, it is worth emphasising that our prominent uniqueness is expressed in public via our unique, rather prominent heads! The head is our most obvious distinguishing feature. Facial recognition software today has become incredibly accurate, even from a distance. Men, in the days when Paul was writing, were more prominent than women and in the religious culture God was still more prominent than Jesus. It was Paul's purpose to teach the revelation of who Christ was and is. He was never reducing the authority, significance or value of Christ, nor was he doing the same for women. Rather, he was speaking into a context where he was introducing a necessary corrective. You can only put forward new thinking when you recognise the point from which you are starting. Paul brilliantly raises his readers' awareness of the prominence of both male to female and God to Christ. Into this he wants to bring a profound revelation in order to establish gender equality, unity and, most profound of all, salvation in Christ. A new society had been inaugurated in which the war between men and women would be defeated by mutual respect, dignity and synergy.

Think back to the Garden of Eden, when Adam and Eve covered their distinctiveness and hid themselves. We suggested earlier that they covered their gender-differentiating features. Now, again, Paul is issuing a challenge regarding distinctiveness. He is encouraging the recipients of his letter to be distinct, male from female. This is not a value statement which implies inequality as much as difference. Celebrating that difference is key to what God wants to do in his Church, still today.

Back to Corinth. In the context into which Paul was writing, men wearing long flowing hair was a sign of homosexuality. Similarly, for a woman to have loose, flowing hair indicated the profession of prostitution, while a shaved head pointed towards forced slavery.[100] These fashion nuances meant that early Christians could be sending a confusing mixed message to the *angels*, or to the community they were trying to win to Christ.

Paul is not trying to oppress anyone. Instead he is trying to bring clarity; to enable the counter-cultural-practices of the early church to be clear. Trying to live a life displaying the gospel is weakened when there is no difference between the believer in Christ and one who is simply following the way of the world. Expressing a difference on the outside will enable the difference on the inside to become apparent.

In his book *Kingdom of Fools*, author Nick Page expands this cultural backdrop and considers that, in this context, the women

Paul writes of are specifically wives. Head coverings were symbols of matrimony, much like a wedding ring is today. A woman who appeared in public with a shaved head was usually being punished for committing adultery.

Men having head coverings was increasingly popular in the culture and context of other religious practices of the day. So, "when Paul writes, then, that Christian men must pray or prophesy with their heads uncovered, at least part of what he's saying is that the church is not to ape the culture of the society around,"[101] Page writes. Furthermore, he acknowledges that "it's Pauline hyperbole, of course, but he's saying that if a married woman takes her head covering off in order to prophesy or pray, she is dishonouring her husband and it's as bad as committing adultery."[102]

Paul writes to encourage the readers to allow for differences between male and female in regard to appearance, such as hairstyles and head-coverings, to ensure they "brought a depth and richness to human relationships that was lost if the genders merely sought to resemble each other. Paul instructs them, then, to affirm the distinction not as a matter of hierarchy or headship (in the sense of authority) but as a matter of relationship."[103]

It is not hard to see how a passage like this has been twisted to dubious ends. With century after century of our male-dominated empire-building tendencies overpowering the Church and creating competition between the genders, we need to ask again, "What does the New Testament really say about all this?" Alan Hewitt points out in *The Gender Revolution*:

"the only place in the New Testament where the word 'authority' is used in respect of a husband and wife is 1 Corinthians 7:4, which says 'the husband has authority over the wife's body, and the wife has authority over her husband's body' (NASB). It is a statement that reflects mutuality in marriage. A point often missed here is that Paul backs up this point by saying specifically that the 'husband does not have authority over his own body but yields it to his wife.'

The salient point here is that in 1 Corinthians 11, discussing men and women in the church, there is more emphasis on mutuality than subordination.

Saying that a man reflects God's glory is not saying that the female doesn't or that she isn't made in the image of God. Here, Paul is drawing not only from Genesis but from the Psalms, where the idea of humans, both male and female being "crowned... with glory and honour"[104] is introduced. If man reflects God's glory, and woman reflects man's glory, is this not another way of saying that women also therefore reflect God's glory? Consider a family scenario where a child is referred to as being "just like" their parent. That child grows up and later becomes a parent themselves. This child of the next generation is also referred to as being "just like" their parent. Surely one can draw the line of understanding that the grandchild must be much like the grandparent? Similarly, the line of created order is simple to understand. Man is made in God's glory and so too is woman, having been made from man.

Many times in the Old Testament men are encouraged to find a wife and the Scriptures encourage the pursuit of a "virtuous and capable wife"[105] to enrich the life of the male. In this letter to the Corinthians, Paul expresses that "man was not made for woman, but woman was made for man."[106] Again, this could sound like the woman is made to be subordinate to the man. However, this is simply poor doctrine. To understand this verse requires a familiarity with the creation narratives. Woman was made as the helper for the man. She came to bring companionship and strength to his weakness. The word *for* could be better translated *because of.* "Paul might rather be saying: 'woman was created because of a need in man... thus woman was created as the strong one to help the weak one.'"[107]

The writer of Genesis understood something profound when writing about man and woman coming together: "a man leaves his father and mother and is joined to his wife, and the two are united into one."[108] Some translations refer to this joining as cleaving. It is widely understood that when one cleaves an item to another, you take the weaker one and join it with something stronger. It is for the strengthening of the original that it is cleaved to another. This concept is not generally understood as bringing strength to the entity to which something is cleaved. Drawing from the full definition of the word *cleave*, of course we understand that it can either mean to join together, as here, or it can mean quite the opposite – to split apart. The possibility of misunderstanding a word with two opposing definitions should not be missed as we evaluate what Paul is really trying to say.

So when considering value between male and female Paul is making reference back to the reality that men needed women. He is radically raising an understanding of the value of women into the context to which he wrote – a context in which women were ignored and largely valueless. Paul is showing that women are, in fact, incredibly valued. He does not want to divide men and women, but rather to emphasise their unity and strength together. We suggest this is not about bringing women *over* men but, *alongside* men. Not *against*, but *beside*; to draw the believers' understanding back to the created order. Ultimately this is not about an abstract sharing of equal value – it is more powerful than that. The New Testament calls us to build on this equality a working synergy that defeats the enemy hands-down.

This becomes apparent when just a few sentences later Paul clarifies further:

"But among the Lord's people, women are not independent of men, and men are not independent of women. For although the first woman came from man, every other man was born from a woman, and everything comes from God."[109]

He could not be clearer. There is an interdependence and synergy between male and female. No one can boast they are the beginning of the chain of creation except God, who was in the beginning. Likewise, no one can become anything other than inter-dependent, united and equal in value across the genders.

Let's move on to chapter 14 of this letter. The contemporary controversy surrounding Paul's teaching on women is furthered when he continues in his letter to the Corinthians that,

"Women should be silent during the church meetings. It is not proper for them to speak. They should be submissive, just as the law says. If they have any questions, they should ask their husbands at home, for it is improper for women to speak in church meetings."[110]

These particular sentences appear in a long message about bringing order into the place of worship, written to both "brothers and sisters" in order to glorify God and help others grow in their faith.[111] It does not stand alone as the only address regarding women. However, this verse is often and too easily used out of context to restrict women and fuel the gender war in the Church.

Some scholars would argue that the scribe has included aspects in these two sentences which Paul never said, because they don't carry the literary flow of Paul's style. Other scholars talk about this being specifically for the people of the context and of no direct relevance to any other subsequent readers. Others would argue that women should indeed never speak in public again! So where is the truth?

We assert that in 1 Corinthians 14 Paul is not speaking about women in general, but about husbands and wives. The implication here is that domestic dialogue needs to be kept in domestic quarters. And, just as a wife was to behave respectfully to her husband and to keep herself righteous by talking at home, so the husband was to keep himself spiritually mature by being able to answer the questions of his wife. This passage is located in a section of the letter which modern translators have titled "Instructions for Public Worship". Paul was committed to taking the message of Christ to the ends of the world. He was personally committed to obedience to ensure the Great Commission was fulfilled. He was addressing matters raised by the Corinthians to respond to particular nuances of disorder that were creeping into the churches, bringing division and threatening their spiritual maturity. Paul does not want the husbands to neglect their own spiritual understanding any more than he wants wives to overstate theirs. It is a symbiotic challenge to be in partnership when married. This advice is worth heeding even today.

Have you ever been in a meeting when a husband and wife bring a personal conversation into the context of a group discussion, or married couples bring personal debate into a place of corporate worship? We have sat around leadership tables where husbands and wives were ministering when a "domestic" has broken out and disagreement ensued. It is unlike any other type of disagreement which can happen amongst believers. We can remember numerous occasions where couples we know have had marital mutterings whilst in a worship context. We've been in meetings where notes have been passed, elbows dug, eyebrows knitted and eyeballs crossed, nostrils flared and feet have been kicked whilst sentences have been truncated by disgruntled spouses! If we were given the opportunity, we too would likely say, "Will husbands and wives please keep their personal disputes at home!" In those cases we too might recommend that wives wait to challenge their husband's motives in the privacy of their own homes. Husbands, would you be ready, and your life in order, to give account to your wives?

Allowing marital arguments into a corporate gathering is an easy way to become distracted from the real reason for the gathering. Obviously there are group contexts where expressing marital problems is highly appropriate and enables an authentic, accountable opportunity for growth and healing. However, this is not the context into which Paul is writing. This is a worship context of mixed gathering, rather than a home-group or marriage counselling session. Paul is writing to urge the believers to keep their focus and enable the main thing to be the main thing. Having wives or husbands chatting through a sermon, giving a running commentary, critique or simply adding questions is highly distracting to everyone else in the place.

Ponder the verses in the letter to the Corinthians again. Paul clearly addresses marital relationships and is speaking more about marital partnership than anything else. He addresses the women and their husbands as "if they (wives) have any questions, they should ask their husbands at home."[112] Ignoring the address to husbands would give room to take the initial instruction to be to *all* women. This is simply poor biblical exegesis. Paul was addressing wives and husbands. He was not applying a general restriction on all who might be called, gifted and anointed to preach and lead.

Paul would have been aware that his words to the church in Corinth would go beyond the group of people listening to it and impact the wider community of believers. However, we think he would have been shocked to know that his letter to the people in the city of Corinth would be immortalised in the Bible, part of the world's most influential book. Furthermore, we're certain he would be deeply grieved to know that two sentences out of context were going to hold back thousands of women (for hundreds of years) from using their God-given gifts in public in the Church.

We have read articles on Paul which have described him as the patron saint of male chauvinism. This is a prime example of the serpent getting close to the centre of God's people in order to keep women restricted. We don't sense that in what Paul wrote, but we *do* hear that in how his writing has been subsequently applied to societies and church structures, leading to gender war and all the carnage that creates. We're not finished with Paul. Next we'll move on to another passage which has unintentionally armed the enemy and brought painful division.

CHAPTER 15
SEEN BUT NOT HEARD? – TIMOTHY

Paul writes to Timothy, his spiritual son:

> "In every place of worship, I want men to pray with holy hands
> lifted up to God, free from anger and controversy. I want
> women to be modest in their appearance. They should wear
> decent and appropriate clothing and not draw attention to
> themselves by the way they fix their hair or by wearing gold
> or pearls or expensive clothes. For women who claim to be
> devoted to God should make themselves attractive by the good
> things they do. Women should learn quietly and submissively.
> I do not let women teach men or have authority over them. Let
> them listen quietly. For God made Adam first, and afterward
> he made Eve. And it was not Adam who was deceived by Satan.
> The woman was deceived, and sin was the result. But women
> will be saved through childbearing, assuming they continue to
> live in faith, love, holiness, and modesty."[113]

Whilst we pick out just a few verses to explore this passage,
we must understand that they are part of a letter. We need to
appreciate where they sit within the whole document. Paul is
writing in response to Timothy, his spiritual son, addressing
some of the challenges he is facing in Ephesus where he is leading
the church. Remember, we are hearing just one side of their

conversation. Timothy is a younger leader who has been called by God to disciple others and Paul is helping him fix the chaos that is arising within their worship context. He is emphasising the significance of prayer and encouraging the believers to pray more, to have more order in their places of worship. There is an apparent rise in false teaching, where Paul has taken a strong line and expelled two people from the church.[114] There was also the cultural influence in Ephesus at the time which was imprinting its mark upon the church, rather than the church rising up as Christ-followers impacting their culture. One particular aspect of the Ephesian culture was the influence of the cult of Artemis "in which the female was exalted and considered superior to the male."[115]

Being in the real world, whilst being distinct from it, is not a new challenge for believers. Paul is trying to encourage the male and female believers to remain distinct and act modestly. The matter of what is worn is significant in order to not attract the wrong sort of attention.

He is addressing the attitude of men to deal with character issues of anger and controversy, in order that they can truly lift holy hands without hypocrisy. Furthermore, he speaks to the attitude of women to be modest and to recognise that real beauty comes from within. Both male and female are being challenged to be pure on the inside in such a way that it becomes visible on the outside. How often do we start at verse nine and forget that, prior to this, man's character and response is also being addressed?

Is it possible that Paul is saying that women should not dress in such a way that they are appreciated only for that – something that should be kept private and intimate? That, rather, they should be appreciated for the children of God that they are? Women are of great worth, so their style of dress should not diminish that. Paul is urging women to be known for their good deeds, rather than their appearance. Being known for what we are on the surface is very shallow, compared to being known for our values, heart and actions.

Clothes were then, and still are now, hugely significant statements of beauty and expressions of dignity. Wearing clothes is so often a personal outward expression for what is on the inside. But as Christans, our hearts and actions should speak louder than our clothes – that we would be known more for our love for the Lord, our vivacious love of life, our loyal friendship, and our gifts and talents. All people, whether male or female, are worth so much that it is sad when their value is cheapened by how they dress. Likewise, it is simply a question of dignity for the wearer and distraction for the observer that Paul is addressing here.

This passage moves on to a sentence that is used to silence women, but should really be used to develop them. Paul writes that women *should learn quietly and submissively*. In the context in which he was writing, women were uneducated and ignored for their learning potential. Paul was bringing value and equality to them by saying, to both men and women, that women should learn! Women should learn! This was a profound awakening to the believers at that time – that women's value was such that they too should be educated.

We see a strategy of the enemy to keep women uneducated that is tragically still prevalent today. In many countries it is the females in society who remain uneducated and restricted. Educate women and you can change a culture. Educate women as well as men and we are becoming biblical believers! In earlier chapters we referred to *Half the Sky*, a book that has inspired a movement. Their campaign should inspire us all to advocate the education of girls and boys to ensure the oppression of women ends. Paul was ahead of our times! He knew that women too should learn.

Submission is not a swear word! It is simply an attitude which we all need if we are going to learn anything. If a student wishes to learn something, they need to submit to their teacher's wisdom, knowledge and experience. To say that women should learn submissively says nothing about value or authority, but simply the attitude which is required. In any learning environment some knowledge is necessary before questions can be asked to gain more knowledge. Students shouldn't expect their teacher to be thrilled by all questions asked if the answer should have been learned the day before in the homework the teacher set! Learning is sometimes best achieved with an attitude of submissive silence. Ask any teacher – the student often needs silence and submission to learn.

Paul is challenging the men to not be arrogant and keep their knowledge to themselves. He tells them to share generously and ensure that the women have equal learning opportunities. Paul is inviting men to be willing to give away their right to be educated alone and instead to empower women with education too. It is much like the heart of Boaz, who gave away not only what was expected but what was generous to the woman gleaning in his field. Furthermore, Paul is challenging the women to not be defensive or arrogant, but willing to learn. It is not simply a case of complaining about what is not available, but rather taking hold of what should be available.

Paul is addressing an imbalance following reports of specific distractions and pride in some women in Ephesus, perhaps inspired by the Cult of Diana.

This is not a restricting verse, but a verse of profound equality, as Paul writes against the friendly fire that is keeping women uneducated. Christianity, in its very essence, was bringing a liberation and value to women and, as such, was counter-cultural and revolutionary. The Church was the forerunner to the manifestation of equality between genders and the Church should still hold this mandate.

However, the verse immediately tumbles into controversy for us as Paul writes, "I do not let women teach men or have authority over them."[116] To really understand this sentence we have to understand the nuances behind each word and how they have been translated, especially the word "authority".

Paul clearly does not restrict all women from teaching, as he permits and affirms the multi-faceted contribution of women in churches which, since they included female apostles, can be understood to include teachers who are female too.[117] Furthermore, from some of his other writings Paul is not universally averse to women teaching. In his letter to Titus he states that Titus should teach the older women to teach; training others, younger women and children. If you take the first part of the sentence only there are grounds to say women can teach. Titus 2:3 says, "Similarly, teach the older women to live in a way that honours God. They must not slander others or be heavy drinkers. Instead, they should teach others what is good."

Some might suggest that it is the teaching of *men* that Paul has in focus. We're not convinced this is a reasonable interpretation given the recognised role of Junia as an apostle (more of that later). Rather, the nuance is in the word that we translate "authority". This is brilliantly developed in the essay by Linda L. Belleville in the collation of *Discovering Biblical Equality*.[118] The emphasis should rather be translated, "I do not permit a woman to teach with a view to dominating a man; or I do not permit a woman to teach a man in a dominating way but to have a quiet demeanour [literally, 'to be in calmness']."[119]

The key is in the word *authority*. Have you ever been in a conversation with someone where you know significantly more than them on the topic being discussed? Perhaps it's a subject you have studied in depth whereas they have never even considered or read anything. The conversation can range from hilarious to infuriating if the one who is uneducated is trying to argue their case without grounding. A parent might smile at the claimed wisdom asserted by their young child who is confidently teaching their parent what they think is unknown to them. A university lecturer might smile at the undergraduate's attempt to present opinion as if learned. Please don't misunderstand us. Of course we can all learn something from everyone. But Paul was addressing a particular challenge. When he was writing to Timothy, the women who were around were largely uneducated. In stark contrast, the men were invested in and educated further. We suggest Paul wanted this to be corrected when he says that women should first learn, submitting to the knowledge of others, before any consideration could be given to them teaching. We know from other passages that Paul was comfortable with women teaching, but not if they had not first learnt what was necessary to be taught.

This is good practice which still applies within church contexts today. Most leaders would not just let anyone preach in their church. They first need to prove that they are qualified and that they have something to say. Not qualification in the sense of being certified by an examination board, but in the sense of proven learning and gifting. Paul furthers this thought to Timothy saying, "keep a close watch on how you live and on your teaching. Stay true to what is right for the sake of your own salvation and the salvation of those who hear you."[120] It is important that those who preach and teach take seriously the responsibility and privilege that is entrusted to them.

Enabling men and women access to equal opportunities and education is foundational to gender equality. It signals the end to gender wars in the church if it can grow into God-glorifying synergy. This is in line with the major trajectory of Paul's teaching – that it is the attitude of a believer which determines behaviour.

Further, it is in line with Paul's understanding of the Creator's plan for men and women to be mutually submissive, mutually equal and mutually called, whilst recognising diversity.

Paul goes on to write that "God made Adam first, and afterward he made Eve, and it was not Adam who was deceived by Satan. The woman was deceived, and sin was the result."[121]

Some have taken this sentence and interpreted it as a hierarchical list of value. However, Paul is not doing anything other than simply recording the order of events and the reality that deception occurred.

That women are going to be saved in childbirth is, of course, an interesting concept. In an earlier chapter we considered the symbolic significance of the pain of childbirth. What does it mean for a woman to be saved in childbirth? Does it mean literally, in terms of physical life? Having had the privilege of having three children, we're not convinced that this was Helen's saving experience! However, we know of global tragic cases when women do lose their lives whilst giving birth.[122] In Paul's time, medicine was less developed and the proportion of infant and maternal deaths would have been far greater. So perhaps this isn't best translated or understood as being physically saved.

One important point to understand here is that by having children, women were continuing their family line, and these children would be the future carers of their elderly parents. Women who were barren were in a terrible predicament, facing abandonment by husbands who might seek more fertile wives. Therefore, they were only *saved* from this by having children.

A stronger argument is that a woman is not saved *by* childbirth but by God's grace saved *through* the pain and risk of child-rearing. However, these theories are very natural and we suggest there is something far more profound and supernatural in Paul's sentence than this. The history of women was that they were "saved" when a man married them and rescued them from their circumstances. Without a husband, a woman was considered worthless. However, Paul is in fact turning this principle on its head and ascribing a greater value to women than would otherwise have been given. Paul wants to emphasise and separate the previously held theories that devalued women, and instead keep teaching the principle that in Christ there is neither male nor female when it comes to the issue of value. Both men and women are saved and given a place in God's family, even through and from the painful consequences of sin.

Previous Jewish understanding would have been that circumcision was the sign of a believer. However, in Christ the sign was no longer circumcision but baptism. Paul is emphasising that it is through Christ that women too are saved, not through their saved husband.

This is a profound statement of equality, value, honour and comes with the condition of the attitude in which the women will live. Namely to live in faith, love, holiness and modesty. It is about receiving the gift of salvation of Christ and living in such a way that the inner reality is seen in the outer fruit.

Paul did not want to restrict women, nor did he want to over-elevate them. He simply wanted to bring an equality of value and honour to both sexes. A synergy in light of his culture-challenging teaching.

Remember our glimpses into the glory of the Garden in Genesis, when man and woman were side by side? There was symbiotic submission and no one ruled over the other. With his understanding of the implications of the curse, Paul is aware of the consequences where the gender battle is fought. But instead of reaching the conclusion that we should be mutually submissive, too often we have supressed women and devalued their gifts. This time the serpent is slithering into the ink of the scribe of this letter and whispering "Did God really say?" to fuel his battle against the woman and her offspring. Paul does not want the authority of one to wield itself over the authority of another inappropriately. Instead we must look at our attitudes to determine our action. Men and women together can only really lift holy hands and show true devotion to God if their inner attitudes are in line with Christ. We must not seek to dominate one another, but teach each other in such a way that Christ is revealed and glorified.

Can we recognise where the battle has become an area of friendly-fire damage and agree to halt, put down our weapons and recognise who the real enemy is? Gifts are given by the Lord regardless of gender, age, race and background. If the Lord so chooses to give women the gift of teaching, and if they are willing to use that gift humbly and without seeking to dominate, then what follower of Christ or student of Paul would seek to get in the way of that?

CHAPTER 16
OTHER NOTABLE WOMEN IN PAUL'S LIFE

We are still with Paul so let's keep going. We are getting there! Can you hear the voice of the Holy Spirit breathing life and revelation? We hope so, as the trumpet sounds for us to stop fighting each other and face our enemy, the devil of division and subjugation. He loves it when we fight, while all of heaven calls for us to make peace and fight the good fight, together.

Paul spent a lot of his time breaking down the boundaries that existed within the Church, communities and societies of his time. He wrote to ensure godly order and Christ-centred discipleship became a reality across the Church in such a way that the community would be impacted. Paul is committed to ensuring the message of the gospel continues to reach the Gentiles and destroys religious barriers with a message of grace and love.[123] Urging the Gentiles to realise they are loved by God, he writes to both men and women[124] to ensure that the message crosses the gender gap and that no one is excluded. He is committed to acknowledging that all have sinned and fallen short, that all are in need of the grace of Christ.[125]

In his letter to the Galatians Paul writes to further remove the barriers that humans build to limit the purposes of God, emphasising, "There is no longer Jew or Gentile, slave or free, male and female. For you are all one in Christ Jesus."[126] The "and" between the words male and female translates from the Greek word *Kai* and is significant in the bringing together both male and female. Paul chooses the phrase "male and female" rather than "neither male nor female" – the pattern he has used so far in these verses – and does so deliberately, because it is the exact phrase used in Genesis 1:27 "male and female he created them". Paul is highlighting the creation narrative and explaining that, in Christ, as Steve Harmon writes in *A Biblical Primer on Women in Ministry,* "the most primary division of God's creation is overcome, that between male and female." Cynthia Long Westfall adds in *Paul and Gender: Reclaiming the Apostle's Vision for Men and Women in Christ,* "the hermeneutics that Paul applied to the Jew-gentile debate can and should be extended to the gender issue."

It is not that Paul does not recognise differences between people, he does on numerous occasions, but he will not have these differences block the purposes of Christ, nor be allowed as an excuse for disunity. Diversity is not a reason for disunity or inequality. It is simply recognition of unique differences. If you want to look further into this we warmly recommend Tim's book, *The Power of One.*

Paul is an articulate communicator and chooses his words carefully and with purposeful precision. At the end of his letter to the Romans, he compiles an honours list of many significant people in his life. The fact that eleven of the twenty eight people honoured are women will have been intentional and profound. In a culture where women were largely ignored, Paul wanted to make sure that, within the Church, they were not. He wanted to make sure that not only was their presence appreciated, but their gifts and contribution also highly valued.

He commends Phoebe, acknowledging her as a sister of faith and holding the rank of what is at least a deacon in the church in Cenchrea. The Greek word used here is *prostatis* which carries clear authority and leadership. In fact, it is the same word that

Paul used to describe his own ministry. He encourages the believers to, "Welcome her in the Lord as one who is worthy of honour among God's people. Help her in whatever she needs, for she has been helpful to many and especially me."[127] What a great commendation, to help her so wholeheartedly, answering any of her requests and holding her in honour. Phoebe was apparently a woman of quality and wealth who had her own business which required her to go to Rome, where she would be a stranger. Paul is valuing Phoebe to such an extent that other believers are to make sure that she does not have any needs. This is profound, as in the culture of that time the needs of women would be ignored as irrelevant, or simply kept within the family setting. Paul brings her needs to the church, however, much like when he would visit and the church met his needs. Paul realises the significance of this woman's contribution as helpful to so many in furthering the gospel. Paul is sincerely commending her as a friend and minister of the gospel and encouraging the believers to extend the warmest of welcomes. Courtesy and Christianity should always be close companions and Paul is honouring her with equal honour to which he would afford a man.

The greetings list in Paul's letter to the Romans continues with him greeting Priscilla and Aquilla.[128] Paul first met this couple when he arrived in Corinth, showing that he was not the first believer there. We read their introduction in Acts: "Then Paul left Athens and went to Corinth. There he became acquainted with a Jew named Aquila, born in Pontus, who had recently arrived from Italy with his wife, Priscilla. They had left Italy when Claudius Caesar deported all Jews from Rome. Paul lived and worked with them, for they were tentmakers just as he was."[129] Tentmakers, Jews and exiled Christians Paul, Priscilla and Aquilla had a lot in common with each other and formed a significant relationship, such that Paul describes them as his "co-workers in the ministry of Christ."[130] As well as tentmakers, Paul's list of gratitude clearly shows that Priscilla and Aquilla both lead a church that meets in their home, filled with Gentile converts. More of that later. In the next chapter we will look in greater detail at the way their partnership is expressed and recorded. It's inspiring stuff.

After mentioning one man, Epenetus, in his letter to the Romans, Paul goes on to greet and honour Mary, Tryphena, Tryphosa and Persis – all women! Tryphena and Tryphosa are understood as the Lord's workers, useful in their mission, and Persis is another good woman who has apparently laboured much in the Lord, more than others, abounding in the work of the Lord.

Paul is determined to ensure that the early Church grasps the truth that the work of women for Kingdom purposes is relevant within a church context. Their contribution mattered to Christ. Women were of equal value in significance and usefulness to the Kingdom, as men were.

Paul also brings greetings for Andronicus and Junia as, "They are outstanding among the apostles, and they were in Christ before I was."[131] The key word in this sentence is *outstanding*. This couple stood out unmistakeably with a marked gift of leadership. This is most likely another married couple who are apparently equally gifted in their ministry, both being recognised amongst the apostles. However, even if they were not married, one thing is clear: Junia is a woman. Scholars have debated whether they were respected *by* the apostles, or *as* apostles. However, the most likely explanation is that they were both apostles. This is a recognised spiritual gift, given by God, where the ability to do the job is also given by God. Paul is acknowledging the fact that there is a female believer called Junia who carries this office. This cannot be done without carrying the burden of great responsibility. Paul is accrediting a woman in a significant role of leadership, influence and authority.

There are other women listed in his greeting, including Junia and Nereus's sister, helping us to see that there were many women in Paul's life, all ministering among the believers, all of whom

Paul was grateful for and whom he went out of his way to honour. Paul was not a chauvinist or a woman-hater. He was, however, a leader of leaders who wanted to address particular issues that these leaders faced.

Paul is first introduced in the Bible as an oppressor and persecutor of the early believers. From the revelation of Christ he then begins a journey of profound leadership, impacting the Church, then and now. As a liberator of the persecuted, his words of freedom include bringing liberty and recognition to women and men with equal measure. He surely never intended division between the genders, but instead sought to bring clarity and godly revelation. He recognised the value of women as equal to men, their need to learn and be educated just as men were, and that their contribution to the Church was as necessary as men's.

Paul is an advocate for life in the fullness of the cross of Christ and far away from the shadow of the curse.

We've made it through. Now surely we must love the Marmite Man a little more and appreciate what he has contributed to our battle-strategy against an enemy who seeks to divide?

CHAPTER 17
FROM 3:16 TO 16:3

Tim writes:

It was probably one of the most profound experiences of my life, there under that rock. I was physically exhausted from the 4,800ft hike from Yosemite Valley to the crest of Half Dome, the signature mountain of California. I had left at dawn and now, four and a half hours later, I was huddled seeking shade from the midday heat. In that refuge I was arrested by the voice of God as I began to write in my journal. I had been reflecting on our leadership journey thus far, asking deep questions after eight years of joys and disappointments. What was next? Then the Lord spoke as clearly as I have ever known, telling me to write:

"You and Helen have been blessed and called to high places. Walk in step with each other. You are called to lead together, love together, parent together, laugh together and witness together. I want you more *together* in life and ministry because the cord is stronger with three strands. My son you need to slow your pace so you can go *together*."

This was not about our marriage as much as our leadership, our collective call, our partnership in the gospel. It was about the beauty and power of *together*. I came down from that mountain with a fresh commission to remember our original invitation: namely that we would serve by leading together.

Eight years later we returned as a family to Yosemite Valley and as I went for a run at dawn, the mist hanging over the meadow as the sun peeked behind Half Dome, I reflected on what God said and the fruit that had already come from agreeing with God in that moment years before. I thank God for *together*.

Let's revisit the grand scheme of God to restore humanity, to recover synergy amongst his people: If the "control and rule" of Genesis 3:16 are the consequences of our sinful rebellion and independence (not how God created us to relate), then we are already encouraged by what we've read. What an inspiration it has been to read from the Old Testament, before the cross, of male-female partnerships that went against cultural norms and overpowered the abuse of power. Deborah and Barak (with the support of Lappidoth), Ruth and Boaz (with the encouragement of Naomi), and Esther and Mordecai (with no help from Haman!) have shown us something of God's kingdom standard in defeating the enemy of division.

All this before the ultimate act of unity – the cross of Christ – where the Father wielded the ultimate sword against the enemy who builds barriers between us.

It's powerful to explore how Jesus turned the tables once-and-for-all in the gender war, and the apostles built the Church on this same foundation. Let's look in more detail at a partnership made in heaven in the early Church. In fact, it's kind of fun that we are stepping from Genesis 3:16 to Romans 16:3 to read a commendation by the great apostle Paul:

"Give my greetings to Priscilla and Aquila, my co-workers in the ministry of Christ Jesus."[132]

Togetherness between men and women is not, as we're showing, limited to a marital arrangement. However, there is something incredibly significant to explore when a marriage is made without any in-fighting. When Paul writes in Ephesians 4 and 5 describing the mutual submission and synchronicity between husbands and wives with respect and dignity, perhaps he has in mind two of his greatest friends, Priscilla and Aquila? Or is it Aquila and Priscilla? More on that in a moment.

Whilst not much is known about this husband and wife partnership, in the seven times they are referred to in the Bible some significant truths can be gleaned. This couple would make fascinating, encouraging, equipping dinner guests. If there is a possibility of a double-date in heaven with these two, count us in!

Dr Luke first introduces us to Aquila and Priscilla in the book of Acts[133] where we learn that Aquila is a Jewish believer married to Priscilla. Her roots are not known, but they have come from Italy where they lived in Rome. Having moved from Italy, the couple are continuing to run their family business as tentmakers. It would seem from Luke's introduction that it was their workplace ministry that first connected them with Paul. He, a tentmaker also, lived and worked with them in Corinth for about eighteen months.

Work with someone for any length of time and you definitely get to know aspects of their character and life. However, when you *live* with someone, the fuller picture of who they are becomes much more apparent. It is hard to hide at home. So with great confidence we understand that Paul got to know this couple very well.

This tentmaking, pastoral, teaching couple risked their lives to take Paul in and help him. In Acts 18 they are introduced to us in the culturally-normative format of the husband being named before the wife. When it came time for Paul to leave Corinth to go on a missionary journey to Syria, Luke tells us that he took Priscilla and Aquila with him. Here is a fascinating observation in Luke's account. When first introduced, Luke follows scriptural and traditional standards, putting the name of the husband first – the cultural norm then and in many places it still exists now. It is a commonly respected sequence that honours and acknowledges the familial name, taken most frequently from the man. However, of the six times that this couple are mentioned in the New Testament, Priscilla's name comes first on four occasions. It seems that Aquila's name is mentioned first only when the reference is to do with their profession or home. Perhaps he was the better tentmaker? However, when the context is the area of ministry it is Priscilla's name that is mentioned first. In his closing greetings to the Romans, Paul lists Priscilla first, arguably on this occasion to honour her spiritual gift as the more significant, or even superior, to her husband's. Nick Page observes, "we shall see from their work in Ephesus, there is a clear indication that Priscilla was the primary teacher of the two."[134] This is not an accident or coincidence; it is a notable inclusion by Paul as he acknowledges that a woman possesses a prominent teaching gift. Far from not wanting women to teach, lead or influence the wider church community, or to restrict them to teaching only women, Paul is acknowledging the strengths and gifts of this apostolic couple to the wider church and, in particular, the role of Priscilla.

Taking Priscilla and Aquila on a missionary journey by sea is a sensible choice. Tentmaking skills are not limited to a standard tent, but are transferable to sails. What's more, it is not an income limited to location, but is widely required and could therefore enable a mission funding stream at sea and in any port or village on the voyage.

However, this couple are not just about their industrious handiwork. Luke continues to explain that the travelling companions parted company temporarily at their first stop in the port of Ephesus. It is here we begin to understand the significance of the couple who were two-*gether* as one.

One leader we've had the pleasure of receiving ministry from is widely respected church-consultant, Joel Holm, formally of Willow Creek. Joel is a wise, strategic communicator who spoke into our church context on one occasion using a phrase that stuck with everyone who heard him. Joel encouraged everyone to "take what they love and make it how they love". In other words, use what you love to do to spread the gospel. We think perhaps Jesus might have said something similar to his disciples when he recruited them, for when he assembled his team he looked at ordinary fishermen and invited them to instead be "fishers of men".

If Priscilla and Aquila were being commissioned and the Scriptures used to prophecy and expand their vision for missional purpose we could imagine the words of Isaiah being used:

"Enlarge the place of your tent,
stretch your tent curtains wide,
do not hold back;
lengthen your cords,
strengthen your stakes.
For you will spread out to the right and to the left;
your descendants will dispossess nations
and settle in their desolate cities."[135]

Priscilla and Aquila were excellent tentmakers but the Lord had an enlarged plan of transformation for them. Perhaps God simply didn't want them to make dwelling places for people – he wanted them to enlarge their vision, enlarge their tent, and expand the very presence of the Kingdom of God on earth. To extend his home on earth, the Church of Jesus Christ. Priscilla and Aquila became co-workers with Paul in the church-planting ministry of Christ, as we read earlier.

We get the first understanding of this enlarged purpose back in the port of Ephesus, when Priscilla and Aquila hear the bold, enthusiastic Apollos teaching about Jesus. They listen to his teaching and whilst it is clearly very enthusiastic and accurate it was limited to an understanding of John's baptism and not the baptism of Christ. So after hearing Apollos, this couple don't go home and have roast-preacher for lunch, instead they invite him to come with them and they teach him what he is missing. Both make tents, both travel, both teach. This couple are completely *two-gether* whilst accepting that her gifts in teaching and pastoring might be the more significant.

Later Paul reunites with Priscilla and Aquila, so when he is writing to the church in Corinth he sends them greetings from the couple. At other times, when apart, he is sure to write sending them greetings.

Paul clearly values this couple incredibly highly, recognising their personal relationship to him as they are said to have both put their lives on the line for him. Furthermore, he recognises their significance to the wider Church of Christ and their part in not only spreading the gospel, but also their dedicated pastoral teaching to help disciples grow in wisdom and stature, as they showed with Apollos.

Priscilla and Aquila are co-workers with each other and co-workers together with Paul. They are both respected, capable, skilled individuals who seem to double their capacity when together. Unlike other couples, they are never mentioned in isolation. There are no examples when only one of them is referenced in their teaching, preaching and leadership, or workplace ministries. They are always together.

We've had to work this out between us, just as most couples have to navigate the path of self-discovery within a partnership. Many couples struggle and fight against losing their independence in a marriage. In our own leadership it sometimes seems more complicated if we are seen as one entity, as "Tim and Helen" rather than playing to our individual strengths. However, for this couple the two seem to have come completely as one. Perhaps in different spheres we can deduce they took turns at taking the lead.

Some scholars go one step further and ascribe the authorship of the book of Hebrews to Priscilla. Why is this only speculation? Because the author of this profound letter (a series of sermons, in effect) is not clear from the text. Some suggest Priscilla's name was withheld in light of the patriarchal structures of authority in the realms of education and even within parts of the Jerusalem-led early Church. Some say the editors and conveyors of Hebrews didn't want the book to lose its place or be taken less seriously because of its female authorship. Interesting theories, with some degree of merit.

What is clear from the book of Acts and other records of the early Church is that Aquila and Priscilla played a key and influential part in the growth of Paul's ministry – a ministry that changed the future of us all. Not only that, they shared workplace and pastoral ministries that carried the hallmarks of a co-equal partnership. Here, in the faltering yet world-changing early years of the Christ-following community, is a couple who are fighting for truth, fighting against the enemies of unbelief and fragmentation between Jew and Gentile, *together*. They fought the good fight without turning on each other.

We have seen in this section some of those who broke through the barriers of self-importance that divides men and women, breaking free from their oppression and suppression by others to lead forward as partners in mission; to fight a common enemy, to fight together. Next we will look to Jesus, our Lord and leader. What can we learn from his life about the battle of the sexes and the future of men and women in his kingdom?

Implications and application – some questions

- What do you find hardest to agree with when it comes to our interpretation of Paul's epistles and the way he addresses male-female relationships and leadership in the Church?

- Is some of this subject matter uncomfortable for you? If so, what further study could you explore to go deeper and clarify your perspectives?
- How would you suggest influencers and leaders in your part of the Church can respond to this section, addressing wrong teaching and inconsistent practice in the body of Christ?

A prayer

All-loving, all-knowing Father, show us your ways today.

In the name of your Son we ask you to remove all the rubbish in our hearts, in our minds and amongst your people, so we might demonstrate on this earth a community of grace, filled with your Spirit.

As a member of your Church, I ask you to forgive me if my life and teaching has not helped others experience the freedom and joy to be who you made them to be. Forgive me if I have allowed my own gender, or the gender of others, to bind up and inhibit rather than serve and release.

Spirit of the Living God, renew me and all your people. Show us the most excellent way of love that we might walk in it.

May we really know the truth and grace of Jesus, the Living Word, our Lord and Saviour.

For your glory,

Amen.

Section 6: Reigning together

As we have been exploring throughout this book, God's agenda with the genders is not to androgenise the human race, removing our differences. He wants to unite us. He wants us to walk, pray, serve and lead together for his purposes. It brings him glory when we stop fighting each other and turn and face our common enemy who has wrought way too much havoc in, and even through, the Church over the generations.

In this final section we want to suggest some ways forward, some victorious steps we can take both personally and corporately, to reverse the effects of the curse in how we relate as men and women in the Church. The result, we pray, will be a stronger society, served and led by a stronger Church – God's kingdom people here on the earth showing what true Christ-centred community can look like.

CHAPTER 18
CONFESSION

As you've read, over the years we have found ourselves in the wrong fight and repeatedly needed to look again and realise who our real enemy is. The Christian life is certainly a battle – a fight of faith in a world of cynicism and confusion. It is also a fight for dignity and equality for all, in a world as divided as ever. We are not to be overtaken or overpowered in these battles, however, because victory is ours in the name of Jesus the Christ. He is our *Christus Victor!*

So this is where the victory in our lives begins: We need to admit defeat; to confess our need for grace and acknowledge our collective guilt. Our real enemy has caused so much damage over the years while men and women have continued the battle of the sexes from generation to generation. We have all, by omission or commission, allowed this battle to rage on and sadly, in the Church we have become so used to competition, point-scoring, comparison and in-fighting that our witness to Christ has been diminished and we haven't made every effort to keep the unity of the Spirit.

Victory begins here. On the knees of confession. At the table of communion, reminded of our sin, yet also reminded of Jesus' covenant faithfulness.

This teaching has fermented like a good wine. It has taken years to write and some of the more painful elements of it we have skirted around before finally moving in and admitting what has really happened between men and women we know whose ministry has been curtailed or polluted, promoted or unrecognised, because of pride, arrogance, insecurity and fear. It is only natural to try and pretend these issues belong to someone else, or that fixing them is someone else's job, when actually we all share the responsibility for building the Church of the future.

We must be honest with ourselves and with others. We wholeheartedly encourage you to take time now to gather your thoughts together, in prayer, and confess to our forgiving God for playing into enemy hands.

James the brother of Jesus writes, "Confess your sins to each other and pray for each other so that you may be healed. The earnest prayer of a righteous person has great power and produces wonderful results."[136]

If we are women who have played into the hands of the enemy and grasped to overpower or undermine, militantly fighting against the men around us or men in general, let's confess our sin to the Lord. We have cast salvos against the wrong enemy. We are guilty of friendly fire. That can change today. This is personal, and we may be able to think of specific people we need to make things right with. Maybe now is the time to confess and to bless.

If we are men who have overpowered and overruled, proudly taken our advantages for granted, and subjugated the women in our lives and women in our world, we must confess our shame and sin. We have played into the hands of our woman-hating enemy and it is time that, in and through our lives, the curse be reversed. With humility we admit our part in the wrong fight and with confidence we can make a change. This is personal and we may be able to think of specific people we need to make things right with. Now is the time to confess and to bless.

If we are part of denominational structures, institutions or organisations that have allowed the gender war to continue, or even added fuel to its fury, we share in the responsibility to make things better for the next generation. Is there a part you can play in challenging those in leadership to make necessary changes to how things are done, to call them to repentance? This is worth thinking and praying about. Perhaps you can take some of the principles in this book and help others to see what the enemy has been up to, so we can turn the battle against him and see our companies and movements enjoying the blessing of greater unity. If you think this isn't for you, then look around at the teams you lead, the platform positions you release, the leadership you release... Are most of the positions filled by men or is there an equal mix?

We are making moves to move from "it wasn't me" to "forgive me, Lord" and the Lord's grace abounds to heal and restore.

We should be inspired and encouraged by the lyrics of Rend Collective that includes the lines, "Your cross, it changes everything" and "When sin and ugliness collide with redemption, beauty awakens."[137]

Perhaps you can join us in this prayer:

Loving God, we thank you for your forgiving grace and daily mercy. We confess our sins to you: our selfishness and pride, our hard hearts and stubborn ways.

Today, in this moment, see that our hearts are for you, and our love is for one another in your Church. We haven't always got things right but now, in response to what you are showing us, we ask for grace to live differently, courage to change our ways, and wisdom to see where the battle lines have really been drawn.

Father, forgive us. Holy Spirit, help and guide us.

Loving Saviour, grant us victory now and always.

For your glory, Amen.

CHAPTER 19
HEALING

Before us there were four leaders serving our church in senior leadership. In the summer of 1998 they all felt called to lay down their leadership responsibilities and fulfil the purposes of the Lord in other ways. Two of them came to see us to tell us their news and asked us an unprecedented question: whether we would be willing to prayerfully consider leading the church. We were not prepared for this. We had never wanted or aspired to church leadership and after Tim finished studying at Bible College he took up employment in graphic design. We had a nine month old baby at the time and Helen's time was dedicated to caring for her. Yet across our lounge the question was posed, "Tim and Helen, will you please consider leading the church?"

Over the course of the next three days of prayer we felt the Lord ask us a much easier question to answer. He asked, "Do you love these people enough to serve them by leading?"

Church leadership had always seemed to us to be a thankless task and not one we particularly wanted or felt qualified for. Yet we loved every person in the small church family we'd been part of for three years. We led the kids' and youth work, knew every family and loved them. So, yes, Lord, we would serve by leading them.

On November 1st 1998 our role began. But somehow, over those few months between the summer and autumn, something interesting happened. The role we were both invited into only ever had a contract, recognition and remuneration for Tim. Perhaps naiveté and parenting priorities for Helen meant that we didn't over-think this at the time and simply walked forwards. We neither asked how much we would get paid nor asked *who* would get paid! We were called together, yet from day one, only one of us was going to be officially recognised and remunerated.

Three years earlier Tim had married a leader. Helen was on the staff of Norwich Youth for Christ and whilst her gift was perhaps only emerging there was a more proven gift and calling on Helen's life than Tim's. He had gained a theology degree (Helen's degree was in Hospitality Management), yet had no increase of ministry experience. It was assumed by everyone that it would be Tim who would give up his role in graphic design, while Helen would keep her stay-at-home-mother role and work for the church in her free time – for free.

A.W. Tozer was famously quoted as saying, "Never trust a Christian leader who does not walk with a limp". Leaders can limp for various reasons and not all of them are bad.

Wounds:

Life can hurt us all in different ways, whether we are male or female. The quest to end friendly fire is not without its pitfalls or fallout. Remember the consequences of the curse which we looked at in the beginning of this book – consequences for the first husband and wife that spill out over all men and women in the struggle of "control and rule"?

We can be wounded when men hold onto power and position so tightly that they won't release opportunities to women. We can be wounded when women strive and grab at position. It becomes like a tug of war to control or rule.

The Psalmist says,

"How good to sing praises to our God! How delightful and
how fitting!
The Lord is rebuilding Jerusalem
and bringing the exiles back to Israel.
He heals the broken hearted
and bandages their wounds.
He counts the stars
and calls them all by name.
How great is our Lord! His power is absolute!
His understanding is beyond comprehension!
The Lord supports the humble,
but he brings the wicked down into the dust."[138]

The Lord longs to rebuild our relationships as a tribute and
testimony to his goodness. If he knows the individual stars by
name, then how much more does he know us and name us? How
ready the Lord is to heal our broken hearts and bandage our
wounds. Are we ready to let him?

If you've ever had an injury you will know that the site of your
injury is extra sensitive and you don't want it touched.

After Helen's lumpectomy she needed further surgery to excise
the area of her leg to check that the cancer had not spread. Whilst
it was good news regarding the cancer being contained after
the second surgery, she picked up a terrible infection in her leg.
Barely able to walk, sit or even lie down due to the swollen and
infected area, Helen's health was under threat. This infection was
going to have to be treated. Infected wounds, left unattended, will
escalate the problem.

Helen writes:

> I didn't want to go back into hospital for yet another week to have further surgery to deal with the infection, but there was little choice available to me. I was taking a shower at home, crying out to the Lord for help when, as I gently rubbed my swollen, sore leg, it became apparent that surgery was not going to come quick enough. The infection in my leg literally erupted. Any teenager who has ever squeezed a spot, simply multiply this by a zillion zits and you'll begin to understand the disgusting scene that unfolded in my shower. Praise God for fresh running water! When I presented myself at the hospital the next day the doctors agreed that the infection had been expelled to such an extent that surgery was unnecessary.

Infections cause limps and need to be dealt with. We need to be honest about the wounds we carry and bring them before the Lord. He is the one who heals and bandages our wounds – all of them. Whether you are a man coming to terms with power-holding or the inadvertent oppression of women, or have struggled with women fighting for their gifts to be recognised. Or whether you are a woman who has been treated unfairly, overlooked or sidelined – we get wounded and the Lord wants to heal us. We can't move forward until we are healed.

Weakness:

Many of us struggle to admit our weaknesses, but until we do we won't recognise that we are strengthened by the help of others. We all need "ezers" to come alongside. More importantly, if we think we can do everything then we are fooling ourselves into believing that we are a whole body rather than a body-part.

The enemy wants us to believe we don't need to admit our weakness, but when we do, then Christ can be revealed within us.

Paul grasped this when he wrote to the Corinthians,

"If I wanted to boast, I would be no fool in doing so, because I would be telling the truth. But I won't do it, because I don't want anyone to give me credit beyond what they can see in my life or hear in my message, even though I have received such wonderful revelations from God. So to keep me from becoming proud, I was given a thorn in my flesh, a messenger from Satan to torment me and keep me from becoming proud. Three different times I begged the Lord to take it away. Each time he said, 'My grace is all you need. My power works best in weakness.' So now I am glad to boast about my weaknesses, so that the power of Christ can work through me. That's why I take pleasure in my weaknesses, and in the insults, hardships, persecutions, and troubles that I suffer for Christ. For when I am weak, then I am strong."[139]

Work:

There are so many things that simply don't come easily to us, but rather have to be worked through. Anyone who has ever gone to the gym or done any exercise will know that muscles gain strength with resistance. When we work through things we get stronger.

This book has taken us, without exaggeration, nineteen years of sharing ministry and nearly ten years of a writing *endurathon*. Friends have read and reread the manuscripts over the years. Many other books have been read. Publishers rejected the manuscript before River embraced it. What started off as a journey that Helen was on, became a journey we were *both* on. This has had to be worked at and for sure we've worked through our limps as we've done so. In Genesis we can read the story of Jacob who wrestled with the angel of Lord and came out limping but with a new identity:

"'Your name will no longer be Jacob,' the man told him. 'From now on you will be called Israel, because you have fought with God and with men and have won.'"[140]

Forgiveness will help us find the faith to persevere to try again, love again.

We can learn something from the prophet Isaiah:

"But as for you, Israel my servant, Jacob my chosen one, descended from Abraham my friend, I have called you back from the ends of the earth, saying, 'You are my servant.' For I have chosen you and will not throw you away. Don't be afraid, for I am with you. Don't be discouraged, for I am your God. I will strengthen you and help you. I will hold you up with my victorious right hand."[141]

The Lord does not throw away those he chooses and loves, but rather will call us back from the ends of the earth

So what do we do now?

Helen writes:

One time Tim and I enjoyed a child-free day off together and decided to head to Windsor Great Park for a day's walk. It was a beautiful day and we thoroughly enjoyed striding out in this stunning royal park. Walking with both silence and conversation interspersed was a wonderful way to spend a day. After a while though, we became self-aware and realised that both our pace and our stride length were identical. We were literally in step with one another. Neither one of us was having to work harder than the other. Neither one was ahead of the other. There was side-by-side synergy.

A prayer

Loving God, we accept your forgiveness for holding onto hurts because we are truly sorry for times when we have kept our wounds, rather than surrendering them into your healing hands. Now we bring to you those painful words, actions and memories that have held us back and caused us to take up arms against people you want us to love.

Heal our wounded hearts, Lord, our healer. Come now into this moment and set us free from anything that hinders us and hurts others.

In Jesus' name,

Amen.

Chapter 20
Synergy - vigilance and diligence

Military tactics are both a science and an art. Countless books, memoirs and movies have demonstrated and celebrated the most cunning, insightful and influential battle-moves of history, ancient and modern. Think of the most moving moments in *Braveheart, Saving Private Ryan, Black Hawk Down* – good tactics and strategic decisions bring victory and save the day. Organising a military force, and the careful use of techniques that combine and use weapons/military units to engage an enemy in battle, especially if they make the most of weather conditions and the shape and state of the environment, is the key to winning or losing any battle.[142]

So we turn to the gender war and ask, what are our enemy's key tactics?

Firstly, fear and insecurity. We have already identified the tragic potential for structures and systems in the Church to reinforce the subjugation and overpowering of women. Matters are made worse when the wrong people end up in board rooms and on church leadership teams, on broadcast television, and in the most powerful pulpits – men holding onto position and failing to ask deep questions about whether the women around them are disqualified because of their gender alone. Where gender comes before gift, insecurity is often the reason why. The enemy loves it when men are afraid to lose their position and when women are afraid to step up and take their place. Our tactics to end the friendly fire need to address this area of insecurity and frailty, on a very personal level, beginning with a right understanding of God's plan for the unity of the sexes and the synergy we have talked about in this book.

Secondly, ignorance and arrogance. Some readers of this book may never get to these latter pages either because they're bored to sleep (we hope not), don't agree with what has been said (we're OK with that), or maybe because they would rather not address the subject head on and admit their ignorance. Our enemy would love to keep our thoughts and theology, our practice and prejudices, in the dark ages – in those dark days of the curse, rather than in the boundless freedom afforded us by the cross. Coupled with that, our enemy loves it when we arrogantly think that our gender uniquely qualifies us and makes us better and more useful than others. We presume to be right and pride divides us. If we are to defeat the enemy, set things right, serve in a more united Church, we must replace our ignorance with awareness and replace our arrogance with humility.

Moving forward in the Church we need to recognise our weak points, like our structural inflexibility and "boys' club" tendencies. When it comes to replacing senior members of our leadership teams and boards, we need to see each transition as an opportunity to select candidates differently; to let gift and calling come before gender.

Another weak point is language. How we describe leaders and their roles may need to change. Way too often we hear the language of "leaders and their wives" and this language has to change! The next generation are growing up taking gender equality as a given, at least much more than they used to, and now is the chance to demonstrate amongst the people of the cross that Christ's work goes beyond equality of value for men and women and calls us to harmonious synergy; the unifying of difference, the strengths of each individual joining for God's glory.

On a basketball court or rugby field, as on the field of battle, peripheral vision is needed to maintain advantage. So too we should stay wide-eyed and aware of our enemy's advances. We need to see him threatening us on every side, on a very personal and interpersonal level, as well as in and through structures and organisations.

As we draw the threads of this book together, the resounding trumpet call for unity and synergy continues with crystal clarity: we must take down the defences between men and women in the Church and keep our defences up against those who try and divide us. A new generation of leaders and influencers must sing a new song of synergy, fostering a culture of mutual celebration and appreciation between men and women. This is not only possible, it is essential. The new society of the Church must show the power of the cross to reverse the curse, even today, and for our relationships to reflect Jesus' heartfelt prayer for his followers.[143] Culture is made up of so many facets – from music and visual arts to drama and the performing arts, governmental structures and education to business enterprises and charitable causes. All of these can be influenced by a Church that has rediscovered a culture of synergy and stopped its self-destructive ways.

A Prayer

Loving God, we thank you for your grace and mercy to us personally and your love for your Church, as well as all those you created.

Forgive us for our divisive, arrogant and insecure ways. We have not always seen ourselves, or each other, as you have seen us.

Give us wisdom and insight. Help us to see the enemy's schemes and defeat them, together, in Jesus' mighty name. Amen.

CHAPTER 21
I'VE GOT YOUR BACK

Over these pages we've walked from the confusing fog of the battlefield, the distress and disappointment of seeing the gender war waged, even amongst God's people, to glimpse Jesus' vision for his people – a community of grace and truth – still being fought over. Jesus' vision for his Church was for leaders and members to love and lead differently than the power structures surrounding them.

It's been a privilege to share some of our mistakes and lessons with you, and some of our ongoing learning as we seek to apply the Scriptures with integrity and honesty in today's world. We've not hidden our scars from you. There have been glimpses here of how our hearts and lives have been scarred from our own skirmishes on the battlefield of gender and power, insecurity and pride. Too often we have forgotten who our real enemy is and found ourselves competing with one another, only to realise our enemy is having a field day.

Even by writing about this subject, we are pulling out of that proverbial cupboard-under-the-stairs some junk you'd rather not sort through. We do not apologise. In fact, we would warmly and strongly encourage you to recognise how unwarranted and useless our proud and arrogant ways are, given the future Jesus has called us to: a glorious future amongst the redeemed community of grace. Grace wins when fear and pride are brought into the light of Christ. As you admit your power-grabbing or power-hoarding ways we trust you are sensing the love and kindness of God to reveal, restore and revive you. That is what we pray for.

Let's not stop fighting, let's just remember who our enemy is.

And let's not just talk a good battle, but really cover each other and be vigilant against our enemy.

Maybe you've had this experience? Close friends-for-life declare they've "got your back" when it comes to protection from enemy ways, and just loyalty in general. However, it seems way too soon that through weakness and misunderstanding, the partnership breaks and it feels like they are actually stabbing you in the back they pledged to protect.

This is a lesson to us – as men and women in God's household – whether single or married, young or not-so-young, we are called to have each other's backs. Not in theory, but in practice. Stand and face the enemy, not with mere words or empty promises, but in prayer and action.

Our hope is that this book will have convinced you of God's powerful plan to reverse the curse and restore synergy between men and women for his great purpose: to extend the Kingdom of God on the earth; to show earth what heaven is like.

Let's live and pray with a wide-eyed commitment to each other and see the fog of war clear in our teams, our homes and congregations, in our denominations and in society as a whole. May the differences among us as men and women no longer be differences that divide us.

A Final Prayer

Heavenly Father, as we have prayed for your grace and forgiveness and the wisdom to walk in your ways, the cry of our hearts is simply this: Let your kingdom come here, as it is in heaven.

May men and women in your Church rise up to champion each other, protect one another, and defend peace and justice.

Holy Spirit, start with me.

Here, now, as I respond to this trumpet call, may I pray and fight for unity, to see the devil of division defeated on every front. In your name and for your glory alone,

Amen.

Epilogue

Helen writes:

My father stood nervously, ready to give his father-of-the-bride speech on August 20th 1994 in a beautiful marquee at our wedding breakfast. He was very accustomed to speaking in public, but not so accustomed to be releasing his daughter to marry her choice of husband. My parents were hoteliers and, as such, had been part of hundreds of wedding receptions in the course of owning their own hotel. At our reception my father joked that never before had he been involved in the preparation and planning of a wedding when the answer to every question was "purple"! Purple is still my most favourite of all my favourite colours!

There are so many stereotypes when it comes to men and women. Blue and Pink have been the respective colours of identification. But this was not always the case. In fact, it wasn't too many years ago when pink was seen as the stronger colour and deemed more suitable for baby boys!

Our culture is demanding redefinition of so many things, urging for clarity on what it is to really be male and what it is to really be female. So many are searching for their identity and are unsure how to identify themselves.

The more people I meet, the more I'm convinced that stereotypes don't work, don't fit, and don't help people be who they are really created to be.

However, the more we wake up to the enemy's strategies, allow the fog of war to be cleared, stop creating victims of friendly-fire and start recognising who are real enemy is, the more we will stop creating victims of the pink or blue and start living in freedom in the beauty of royal purple!

We are not meant to be the same as everyone else in our culture. As Bible-believing, God-fearing Christians we are meant to be set apart. We should not be catching up with society, but taking a lead. Let's live as our Father God intended us to live and let the world see.

Peter writes,

"But you are not like that, for you are a chosen people. You are royal priests, a holy nation, God's very own possession. As a result, you can show others the goodness of God, for he called you out of the darkness into his wonderful light.

Once you had no identity as a people; now you are God's people. Once you received no mercy; now you have received God's mercy.

Dear friends, I warn you as 'temporary residents and foreigners' to keep away from worldly desires that wage war against your very souls. Be careful to live properly among your unbelieving neighbours. Then even if they accuse you of doing wrong, they will see your honourable behaviour, and they will give honour to God when he judges the world."[144]

End Notes

1. http://en.wikipedia.org/wiki/Fog_of_war (last accessed 27/7/14)

2. *Half the Sky*, Nicholas D Kristof & Sheryl Wudunn, Virago, p.xxiv

3. *Half the Sky*, Nicholas D Kristof & Sheryl Wudunn, Virago, p.xviii

4. *Half the Sky*, Nicholas D Kristof & Sheryl Wudunn, Virago, p.159 (brackets mine)

5. Genesis 3:14-19

6. Genesis 1:28

7. Ronald W Pierce and Rebecca Merrill Groothuis, *Discovering Biblical Equality*, IVP Academic p13

8. Genesis 1:10; 1:12; 1:18; 1:21; 1:25

9. Genesis 1:31

10. Genesis 1:21

11. Genesis 1:26

12. Genesis 2:7

13. Genesis 2:15

14. Genesis 2:17

15. Kris Vallotton, *Fashioned to Reign*, Chosen, p44

16. Kris Vallotton, *Fashioned to Reign*, Chosen, p44

17. Kris Vallotton, *Fashioned to Reign*, Chosen, p45

18. Kris Vallotton, *Fashioned to Reign*, Chosen, p46

19. Genesis 2:24

20. Genesis 2:18

21. Derek and Dianne Tidball, *The Message of Women* (Inter-Varsity Press 2012) p36

22. Genesis 3:6

23. Genesis 3:7

24. Jenny Baker, *Equals*, SPCK, p28

25. Genesis 3:21 NLT

26. Isaiah 61:10 NLT

27. Genesis 3:14 NIV

28. Kris Vallotton, *Fashioned to Reign*, p21, Chosen

29. Matthew 1:18 NLT

30. Galatians 5:7

31. Hosea 14:9 NLT

32. Genesis 3:16 NLT

33. Genesis 3:19 NLT

34. Ephesians 6:12

35. Ephesians 6:10-20

36. Ephesians 6:11
37. Nehemiah 4:23
38.www.churchofengland.org/prayer-worship/worship/book-of-common-prayer/at-the-burial-of-the-dead (accessed 25/9/14)
39. John 1:12-13 NLT
40. Genesis 1:27-31
41. http://www.behindthename.com/name/deborah
42. Judges 4:1-4
43. Judges 4:6b-10
44. http://christianity.about.com/od/oldtestamentpeople/a/Barak.htm
45. Judges 4:4 NLT
46. Judges 5:1ff
47. Ruth 1:16-17
48. Ruth 3:10
49. Ruth 2:6
50. Lev. 19:9-10, 23:22; Deut. 24:19-22
51. Ruth 2:15-16
52. Ruth 2:20
53. Ruth 3:7
54. Ruth 3:9
55. Ezekiel 16:8
56. Ruth 4:18-22
57. Matthew 1:1
58. Matthew 1:5
59. Matthew 1:16
60. Psalm 16:3
61. Esther 1:3-6
62. Esther 1:9
63. Esther 1:11
64. Esther 1:22
65. Esther 2:2
66. Esther 2:5-7
67. Esther 2:9
68. Esther 2:10
69. Esther 2:20
70. Esther 4:13-14
71. Esther 4:15-16
72. Esther 4:17
73. Isaiah 9:6-7
74. John 3:16-21

75. John 14:6
76. John 15:1
77. Luke 1:44
78. Luke 2:25-40
79. Kenneth E. Bailey, *Jesus through Middle Eastern Eyes*, SPCK, p202
80. John 4:32
81. Luke 4:25-27
82. Kenneth E. Bailey, *Jesus Through Middle Eastern Eyes*, SPCK, p194
83. Luke 13:18-20
84. Luke 10:40
85. Luke 10:39
86. Kenneth E. Bailey, *Jesus through Middle Eastern Eyes*, SPCK, p194
87. Luke 10:41-42
88. Luke 8:1-3
89. Kenneth E. Bailey, *Jesus through Middle Eastern Eyes*, SPCK, p193
90. Matthew 26:55-56; Matthew 27:55-56
91. Mark 15:40f
92. Matthew 28:7
93. Kenneth E. Bailey, *Jesus through Middle Eastern Eyes*, SPCK, p198
94. David Williams, *Junia, a Woman, an Apostle*, p153
95. Galatians 3:27-29
96. Genesis 3:1 (NLT)
97. Conrad Gempf, *How to Like Paul Again*, Authentic, p23
98. 1 Corinthians. 11:3-16
99. Alan Hewitt, *The Gender Revolution*, River Publishing, pp106-7
100. Derek and Dianne Tidball, *The Message of Women*, IVP, pp214-215
101. Nick Page, *Kingdom of Fools*, Hodder & Stoughton, p230
102. Nick Page, *Kingdom of Fools*, Hodder & Stoughton, p230
103. Derek and Dianne Tidball, *The Message of Women* (Inter-Varsity Press) p218
104. Psalm 8:5
105. Proverbs 31:10-11
106. 1 Corinthians 11:9
107. Derek and Dianne Tidball, *The Message of Women* (Inter-Varsity Press) p217
108. Genesis 2:24 NLT
109. 1 Corinthians 11:11-12
110. 1 Corinthians. 14:34-35
111. 1 Corinthians 14:6
112. 1 Corinthians 14: 35

113. 1 Timothy 2:8-15

114. 1 Timothy 1:20

115. Linda L. Belleville: *Teaching and Usurping Authority* in Ronald W. Pierce and Rebecca Merrill Groothuis, *Discovering Biblical Equality*, IVP Academic, p219

116. 1 Timothy 2:12

117. Romans 16:1-16, v7 ref Junia the apostle

118. Linda L. Belleville: *Teaching and Usurping Authority* in Ronald W. Pierce and Rebecca Merrill Groothuis, *Discovering Biblical Equality*, IVP Academic Ch12

119. Linda L. Belleville: *Teaching and Usurping Authority* in Ronald W. Pierce and Rebecca Merrill Groothuis, *Discovering Biblical Equality*, IVP Academic p219

120. 1 Timothy 4:16

121. 1 Timothy 2:13-14

122. www.who.int/mediacentre/factsheets (World Health Organization)

123. Romans 1:6

124. Romans 1:13

125. Romans 3:23

126. Galatians 3:28

127. Romans 16:1-2

128. Romans 16:3

129. Acts 18:1-3

130. Romans 16:3

131. Romans 16:7 NIV

132. Romans 16:3

133. Acts 18: 2-3

134. Nick Page, *Kingdom of Fools*, Hodder & Stoughton, p195

135. Isaiah 54:2-3 NIV

136. James 5:16 NLT

137. By Rend Collective from the album *Homemade Worship from Handmade People*, Integrity Music, 2012

138. Psalm 147:1-6

139. 2 Corinthians 12:6-10

140. Genesis 32:28

141. Isaiah 41:8-10

142. For links to some fascinating books and articles about military tactics, try https://en.wikipedia.org/wiki/List_of_military_tactics

143. John 17:20-21

144. 1 Peter 2:9-12 (NLT)